Warneford, VC

Warneford, VC

by Mary Gibson

FRIENDS OF THE FLEET AIR ARM MUSEUM
1979

First published in 1979 by The Fleet Air Arm Museum
Royal Naval Air Station, Yeovilton, Somerset BA22 8HT
for the Society of Friends of the FAA Museum

Edited and designed by Colin & Barbara Huston
Printed in Great Britain by
A.B. Printers Limited, Leicester

ISBN 0 906891 00 0

Foreword

by Admiral of the Fleet Sir Caspar John, G.C.B.

From his early days Rex Warneford was something of a loner and able to make up his own mind.

This led him round the world in various occupations on land and sea, ending in his learning to fly and joining the Royal Naval Air Service as an aircraft pilot early in the first World War.

This book, written by a cousin, Mrs Mary Gibson, tells the story of his life, finishing with the exploit which brought him fame — the destruction, in the air, of Zeppelin LZ37, the first such occurrence, together with his immediately subsequent forced landing in enemy territory and resourceful escape flight to a friendly airfield.

The successor to the Royal Naval Air Service is the Fleet Air Arm, in which a man of the skill and courage of Rex Warneford would have been very much at home.

His inspiring example is recorded in the Fleet Air Arm Museum at the Royal Naval Air Station, Yeovilton, Somerset, alongside those of many other men of his high calibre.

Caspar John

Acknowledgements

It would have been difficult to write this biography without the generous assistance of various members of the Warneford family, including Rex's sisters Mrs Jean Doddington, the late Mrs Dorothy English and Mrs Vi Black; also his aunt the late Mrs Katharine Sibley, his cousin Mrs Winifred Loraine, and my sister Mrs P Gubbins.

Others who have supplied valuable information or pictures include Olive, Lady Antrobus, the late Miss Evelyn Banbury, the Rev E R Chesterton, the late Albert E Hawkins and Mrs Hawkins, Mr & Mrs J S Kinross, Miss M B Pitman BSc, Mevrouw H Smit-Donkersloot, Major J Wilson and the late Mother Superior of the Convent of St Elisabeth, Ghent: I am most grateful to them all.

My thanks also go to N S Pratt MA, Headmaster of King Edward VI School, Stratford-upon-Avon; the Rev Ernest Johnson, Rector of Satley, Co Durham; Anthony Grover (Chairman) Lloyd's Register of Shipping; E M Smith, British India Steam Navigation Co Ltd and John Szemerey, P&O Orient Lines for many particulars of Rex's early years; to Commander T A Marshall RN, Herr K Puzicha (Marineluftschifferkameradschaft Hamburg) and John Prebble for information on his service period; and to R G Gray and the J M Bruce/G S Leslie and World Ship Society Collections for additional photographs.

I am also indebted to the late Sir Arthur Longmore for permission to quote from his autobiography *From Sea to Sky*, to T Batsford & Co for quotations from *First Through the Clouds* by F W Merriam, and George G Harrap & Co for passages from *Monsters of the Purple Twilight* by Ernest Dudley.

For their kind advice and assistance or photographs I must express my gratitude to the officials and staff of the following organisations: The Admiralty Historical Branch; Ministry of Defence Library; Imperial War Museum; Royal Air Force Museum; Fleet Air Arm Museum; Public Record Office; British Newspaper Library; Foreign Office Library; India Office Records; Belgian Embassy London; Chilean Embassy London; French Embassy London; High Commission of India; Archief Stad Ghent; Musée de l'Armée et de l'Histoire Militaire, Brussels; École d'Artillerie Anti-aérienne, Brussels; Bibliotheek Katholieke Universiteit, Nijmegen, Netherlands; Archivos y Museos, Santiago de Chile; and the editors of *Het Volk*, Ghent and Wiltshire Newspapers Ltd.

Last but not least I must acknowledge the diligent researches of Major William Naesmyth RA, who uncovered many facts, and Patricia Vernon Watson who encouraged me to complete the manuscript, then devoted many hours of loving labour to typing the result.

Special thanks are due to Commander D C B White, OBE RN (Retd), Director of the Fleet Air Arm Museum, who provided the enthusiasm and driving force to have this biography published, and my greatest gratitude to Colin and Barbara Huston, who, with assistance from other members of Cross & Cockade Great Britain, undertook with untiring dedication the final editing and design.

M.G.

September, 1979

Contents

Foreword by Admiral of the Fleet
Sir Caspar John, G.C.B.   5

Author's preface   9

chapter one   Indian Interlude   11

chapter two   The Cooch Behar Railway   18

chapter three   Goodbye India   23

chapter four   School Days   27

chapter five   To the Pacific and the Orient   31

chapter six   Hospital in Calcutta   38

chapter seven   The SS Mina Brea   42

chapter eight   A Period of Training   51

chapter nine   Warneford Place   57

chapter ten   The Aerodrome at St Pol   61

chapter eleven   The Zeppelin Menace   70

chapter twelve   Fire over England   78

chapter thirteen   The End of the LZ37   82

chapter fourteen   Mission Accomplished   94

chapter fifteen   Paris   103

chapter sixteen   Come, Winged Death   112

chapter seventeen   Those Whom the Gods Love   118

Bibliography   125

Index   126

Whom the Gods loved they gave in youth's first flower
One infinite hour of glory. That same hour,
Before a leaf droops from the laurel, come
Winged Death and Sleep to bear Sarpedon home.

Iliad xvi. 676-683

Knight's Cross of the Legion of Honour. Reverse showing damaged enamel.

Author's preface

Reginald Alexander John Warneford, the young airman hero of the first World War, because he destroyed a German Zeppelin single-handed, became for a short while the most famous man in the world. His name still echoes faintly wherever acts of bravery in the air are recalled.

Delving back into the origins of his forbears we discover with surprise that he came from a long line of parsons, musicians, and poets. He was an enigma to his fellow men, to whom he appeared foolhardy and carefree, and they frequently misjudged him. He went on his way, a law unto himself, shy, reserved, deeply committed to his own private code, with no concern for his personal safety. He abhorred publicity. The notoriety which hounded him after his encounter with the airship became an almost unbearable embarrassment to him. He feared no responsibility, and having found the key to his own character, his judgement of others was fair.

This story of his short life has been written to give as clear a picture of him as possible, and explain the circumstances which shadowed his death.

1

Indian Prelude

The life of Reginald A J (Rex) Warneford was greatly influenced by his father, Reginald William Henry Warneford, and his grandfather, the Rev Thomas Lewis Warneford, both of whom had lived the major part of their time in India, either serving with the British Army or involved in adventurous work during the great days of the British Empire.

The Rev Thomas Lewis Warneford spent 25 years in India as an army chaplain on the ecclesiastical establishment of the Bengal Army from 1866-1891, having left the country parish of Piddletrenthide in Dorset when he was 33 years of age. After a particularly hazardous voyage around the Cape of Good Hope in the sailing vessel *Roxburgh Castle* he landed at Calcutta on December 5th, 1866. He travelled with his young and delicate wife, and their two children; his seven year-old son Reginald and his daughter Maude who was only two. A very short time after Tom had taken up his post as chaplain to the military station at Dum Dum, his wife Charlotte died of cholera. She had been taken ill during the long sea voyage, and the climate of the unhealthy delta had rapidly consumed her remaining strength. As Tom followed her coffin to the dusty English cemetery in Calcutta he blamed himself bitterly for bringing her out to India.

Life became meaningless without her, every place in the bungalow reminded him of his loss. In the end he could not bear it any longer and asked to be relieved of his post and sent to minister elsewhere. Almost immediately his request was granted and he sailed for the Andaman Islands far out in the Bay of Bengal. These beautiful islands served as a penal settlement for Sepoy mutineers captured after the Indian Mutiny. The barracks which housed these men were located on South Island, Viper Island, Chatham Island, Hope Island and Ross Island where the headquarters were situated. Tom Warneford as chaplain to the settlement occupied a bungalow at Port Blair on Ross Island. Conditions there were extremely grim, the officers of the English garrison lived like petty princes, graft was rife and the administration corrupt. General Donald Stewart, one of the heroes of the Mutiny, had been sent out to the Islands in the position of Superintendent to bring order out of chaos. He was present when, on the evening of February 8th, 1872, the Viceroy of India, Lord Mayo, was assassinated by a prisoner from the Punjab on the shore at Hope Island.

Tom's children spent their childhood on the Andaman Islands. Their bungalow was staffed by prisoners on parole and the children looked on these unhappy men as their friends, and had no fear of them. Reginald and his sister grew up as free as the native fisher children with whom they played. They ran wild, climbing the steep hills which dominated Port Blair, from where they could see the many green islands lying like emeralds in a sapphire sea. They swam like turtles in the clear water of the sound, out to the coral reefs where they dived for rare shells which they brought back to swell their father's collection. Tom was an enthusiastic conchologist and the best specimens of his collection can still be seen in the Natural History Museum in London.

Soon after the tragic event of Lord Mayo's death General Donald Stewart returned on furlough to England. Tom, now back in Calcutta, wrote in his journal 'When I was leaving the Andamans I received a letter from General Stewart asking if I would join the Southern Afghanistan Field Force as chaplain. Three days settled the matter, and I received a telegram from Adjutant-General Lumsden telling me to join General Stewart's force at Umballa without delay. The march to Quetta took some time, and when we reached there we found General Stewart had gone on to Kandahar. As soon as the convoy started I was again on the march, and joined the general. An extract from General Stewart's diary reads: 'Warneford has just come in looking the picture of a brigand in a khaki suit, long white boots, and a beard.' Tom remained with the Afghanistan Field Force the whole term of Donald Stewart's command.

He was at Kandahar throughout a severe outbreak of cholera. Then later, at Christmas 1879, no one in Kandahar knew that an order for the march of his division from Kandahar to Kabul was about to be issued to General Stewart. So again Tom was ready for adventure.

From January 1st, 1880 he kept a brief diary of events, recording vividly the now nearly forgotten march to Kabul, during the progress of which the Battle of Ahmed Khel was fought, and the fortress of Ghani was occupied. Tom Warneford accompanied the force throughout this march, and was active in helping to save a tricky situation when the 2nd Afghanistan Field Force was cut off by Ghazni tribesmen at Ahmed Khel, for which act of bravery he was awarded the Medal of Ahmed Khel with Clasp, and was twice mentioned in despatches.

'During this engagement', wrote General Stewart in his dispatch, 'which lasted a short death-packed period, Warneford, mounted on his white pony, was everywhere in the thickest of the fight, calling to the men to stand fast. He actually took the initiative when some of our officers were cut down to lead the men forward, thus turning the battle to our advantage in one of its most critical moments. The Afghan advance was stayed, they turned aside to our right rear in full retreat seeking a way to escape from the murderous fire of our infantry. In a matter of moments they were gone, leaving their dead and wounded lying in heaps within a few feet from where we stood.'

The final history of the North Afghanistan Field Force is too long to include here. Tom Warneford remained as chaplain, until it left Kabul, and returned to India by the Khyber in the autumn of 1880. He was due for leave, and as his son Reginald was 13 years old he decided it was time for both his children to be educated in England. They did not look forward to leaving the country which they had come to regard as their own. They could speak Hindustani and other Indian dialects like their mother tongue. Half-way through the voyage home Tom took them ashore at

Alexandria where they saw Pompey's pillar, and raced along the length of Cleopatra's Needle as it lay on its side awaiting shipment to England.

They stayed for a few days in London, and then were taken by their mother's brother to a house in Hampshire where a clergyman and his wife ran a preparatory school for boys. Here they were separated, their father and Maude returning to London, Tom to take up his ministry in India again, leaving Maude with her aunt. Reginald's life was made a burden to him from the start. The six other boys at the school aged from eight to 14 years old mimicked his clipped English, jeered at his stories about India, and nicknamed him 'Darkie'. He hated them all. They bullied him and waylaid him and never left him in peace. He fought back like a tiger, tooth and claw. They said he did not fight fair; he probably did not, according to their standards, having learnt wrestling from the fisher boys on the Andaman Islands, against which skill his tormentors had no defence.

After a year he was sent on to Rugby where again he found it difficult to fit in. All of his eight years of 'exile', as he called it, had but served to strengthen his passionate love for India. At the end of this time Tom came back to England and shortly afterwards they both set sail again for India. Reginald kept to himself during the journey out, moody, waiting, his eyes straining towards the east which day by day drew nearer. 'Everything comes alive again' he wrote to his sister, 'I feel I have been dead these last years. Each day the distance shortens between me and home. I can hardly bear to wait until this ship moves up that treacherous Hoogli and I set foot once more on the land which means so much to me.'

Tom was anxious that his son should take up a military career, and, on the advice of General Sir Donald Stewart, had bought for Reginald a commission in the Oudh Volunteers. Reginald joined the regiment on his 21st birthday, very reluctantly, as he had hoped to be allowed to attend a technical school of engineering. When he took time off from his military duties he was most usually to be found at the houses of the Indian intelligentsia around Calcutta, much to the disapproval of his father. The upshot of this was, that Reginald found himself transferred to the Northern Bengal Mounted Rifles stationed at Darjeeling. Surprisingly he took to this change better than was expected. He loved the surrounding country, the riding, and the exhilaration of climbing the far-flung ridges of snow-peaked mountains. With all this he might have been satisfied had not fate taken an unexpected twist. One evening he met the lovely Alexandra Campbell, nearly 17 years old. She was the daughter of Captain Campbell DSO, and had not long since come out from England.

Reginald's life was that of a solitary batchelor, of slender means. He thought time was wasted at the bridge parties, the dances and other social engagements of the English community. One day he was reprimanded by his Colonel for avoiding the local activities, and was ordered to put in an appearance at a forthcoming regimental dance. This was where he first set eyes on the lovely Alexandra, floating by in her swirling white ball dress in the arms of one dashing young officer after another. Her programme was filled as soon as she set foot in the ballroom. Reginald could only watch hopelessly, and wish for the first time in his life that he had taken dancing lessons. There seemed to be no chance of extending his acquaintance with Alexandra Campbell any further, but by chance he did just that.

One early morning before the first mists had cleared away, he was exercising one of his chargers with his syce, when he heard the sound of galloping hooves approaching him down a steep hill. Round a bend in the road came a pair of bolting ponies attached to a lurching pony trap, driven by a frightened girl pulling helplessly on the reins. It was Alexandra Campbell! When they were almost on him, Reginald flung himself off his horse, jumped into the path of the runaway pair, and dragged them to a standstill. A dishevelled and tearful Alexandra almost fell into his arms. The ponies stood, heads lowered, breathing heavily, their wild spirit evaporating from their distended nostrils and heaving flanks. Reginald instructed his syce to take his horses back to the barracks, and mounting to the box seat of the cart he drove Alexandra to her father's house.

The result of this dramatic encounter was predictable. She fell head over heels in love with her rescuer. She was a highly emotional girl, and when Reginald proved himself an ardent suitor, even though he could not dance, she was determined to marry him. Captain Campbell was grateful to the young officer for saving his daughter from a nasty accident, but his gratitude did not go as far as wanting him for a son-in-law. When Reginald approached him to ask for the hand of his daughter, the answer was a very determined NO. The refusal did little to damp down Reginald's determination to marry Alexandra, and the romance flourished all the brighter for the opposition it encountered.

At this time there was a growing need for more and more railways in India to link up distant cities and villages with the main lines already in use. His Highness the Maharajah Bhup Bahadur of Cooch Behar issued a proclamation to his subjects after his accession, with the following announcement... 'Being anxious to connect our capital with the railway systems of Bengal, we contemplate measures for the construction of a railway to Gitalda.' The scheme had been in hand for six years, and so far with no successful outcome. In January 1883, Major Engeldue, the then chief engineer of the project to connect Cooch Behar with the line to Mogulhat, inspected the proposed route. An estimate for a $2\frac{1}{2}$ foot gauge railway to be laid over an existing country road was prepared and submitted to the government. In anticipation of the work being put in hand, the embankment for Kalligat was begun but never completed.

His Highness in council decided to re-open the project, abandoned because of flooding and trouble with the work gangs who had a habit of disappearing back to their villages as a passive protest against the overseers and English engineers. Later, with a new staff, work was recommenced on another embankment which also shortly collapsed, this time with considerable loss of life. Another series of earth works was thrown up only to be washed away during the next rainy season. Mr Furnival, an agent for the Bengal Central Railway made his report, and on this being received the whole scheme was put into abeyance for five years, when it was decided that it should be abandoned. This was where Reginald came into the picture.

After nearly six years in abeyance, tenders were again put out to discover any engineer who could beat the natural hazards of the terrain, and build the railway. Reginald with little theoretical knowledge, and no practical experience whatever, applied for the position of chief engineer to the Cooch Behar Railway, and got it.

H.H. Nripendra Narayan Bhup Bahadur, Maharajah of Cooch Behar 1862-1911.

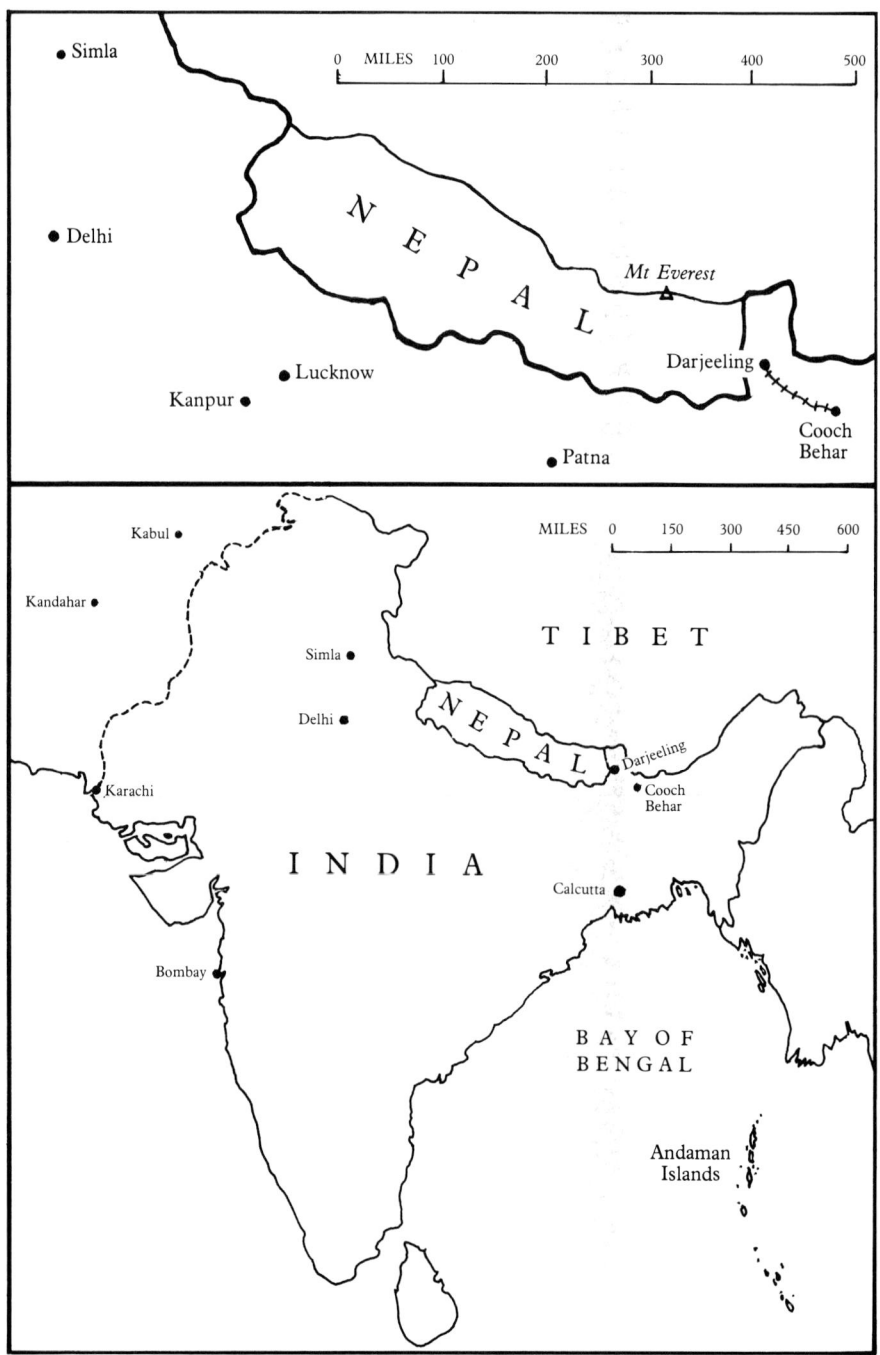

Simla

Delhi

NEPAL

Mt Everest

Lucknow
Kanpur

Darjeeling
Cooch
Behar

Patna

Kabul

Kandahar

Simla

TIBET

NEPAL

Delhi

Darjeeling
Cooch
Behar

Karachi

INDIA

Calcutta

Bombay

BAY OF
BENGAL

Andaman
Islands

He was 28 years old when he resigned his commission with the Northern Bengal Mounted Rifles and took up his abode in the derelict works bungalow abandoned by his predecessors. Standing on the bare boards of this tumbledown shack he felt more at home than at any time since he had landed in Calcutta. He spent the first few days on the job interviewing the Indian foremen, the natives who were to do the pick and shovel work, and two Indian engineers who had come up from Calcutta.

In two months he had exchanged the works office for a fine new bungalow which combined both an up-to-date office and his own living quarters. In this way it would be easier to keep his finger on the complexities of the scheme and be more easily available to his work force. Every possible inducement and assistance was put at his disposal and he was now rich beyond his wildest dreams. The time was ripe to face Captain Campbell with his infinitely improved situation, and prove that he could keep Alexandra in the way of life to which she was accustomed. Faced with the facts and the renewed pleading of his daughter, Captain Campbell could no longer find any argument to refuse his consent to their marriage, which took place with full military honours on September 3rd 1890.

Alexandra Campbell

2

The Cooch Behar Railway

Everyone knew that the courtship had been fraught with doubts and difficulties, but nothing clouded the joy and hope in Reginald's and Alexandra's eyes as they set off on their honeymoon. It was all too short. Reginald received an urgent message that he was needed back at the railway site without delay. Alexandra, although put out, followed him like a lamb.

She was delighted with everything that she found in her new home: her pretty drawing room, the salaaming servants, and outside on the gravel drive a new pony phaeton with a pair of beautifully matched ponies. A turbaned syce was to accompany her. Reginald would never allow her to drive out alone. There was however one fly in the ointment. Alexandra soon found out that she must share her husband's company with the Cooch Behar Railway, a very demanding mistress. Although he protested that he was never happy for a moment when he was away from her, she had a very shrewd impression that once engrossed in his work he forgot her completely.

The first rails were laid on the south side of the Torsa river opposite the town of Cooch Behar, in the spring of 1891. Before this could be achieved, however, there were the hard winter months to surmount when the workmen had to labour under very perilous conditions ballasting the permanent way, blasting through the steep slopes of hills covered with thick jungle growth, shoring up embankments, and finally laying the heavy sleepers.

Alexandra, homesick for the gaieties of Darjeeling and left to herself in the new bungalow, began to fret. There were no parties at Cooch Behar where she could show off her pretty gowns, and while she could drive out in her pony phaeton there was no one she wished to call upon, and worst of all no European girls with whom to exchange confidences. To make amends Reginald showered her with expensive presents; jewels, cut glass flagons of French scent, and amusing bibelots to decorate her dressing table. They remained very much in love, the quarrels which blew up from time to time being only small storms in a teacup, which made inevitable reconciliations doubly sweet.

On October 15th, 1891, their first child was born. Reginald's happiness was complete. He had a son, his railway building was going ahead with success in sight, money was now no problem, and to crown everything he had his lovely Alexandra. The baby boy was given three Christian names; Reginald, after his father, Alexander, as a compliment to his maternal grandfather, and last but not least John, after his other grandfather Warneford. Sadly though, before he was six months old, dissension began to cloud the peace of the young couple's home.

Alexandra resented her husband's friendships with members of the local Indian community whom he occasionally invited to dine with him. Alexandra did not refuse to act as hostess to her husband's guests, but she did not manage to conceal her aversion. Before her second child, a daughter, was born a rift in the marriage became apparent. She frequently returned to her parents' home for longer and longer visits, although she was too proud to admit that her marriage had been a sad mistake.

Reginald (2nd from left) and Alexandra Warneford (centre) at a Darjeeling garden party.

Inexorably Reginald's railway track snaked its way over deep ravines following the trail which had previously been the only link between widely separated villages and the outside world into Bengal. Great quantities of heavy timber were brought up by mules, and the bright new rails sent out from the steel mills of Great Britain were tied into place. High stone-faced embankments were constructed to strengthen the sides of the cuttings, and to channel the mountain streams. Spindly bridges were first thrown across deep gulleys, and heavier ones made of cast iron spanned the wider rivers of the plains. These were then strengthened to take great weights or they would have collapsed when the rains caused the streams to become raging torrents.

The first stretch of the permanent way was completed on September 15th 1893, and the line was opened for goods traffic. The whole town turned out on this momentous occasion; among the important dignitaries awaiting the arrival of the first train was the Rajah of Cooch Behar himself, enthroned in state on the new station's platform. Reginald Warneford rode on the footplate of the engine all the way, deeply concerned over this test on a track which had previously only supported construction trucks pushed by workmen and pulled by mules. But the jinx which had haunted the project of the Cooch Behar Railway had been finally dispelled. The link was now forged between the State and the outside world. There followed a day's celebrations in the town, and a State Banquet at the Palace which Reginald and his wife attended. Alexandra entered the banqueting hall on her husband's arm, wearing a full-skirted ball dress, elbow-length kid gloves on her lovely arms, and a diamond aigrette in her hair. After this Reginald found himself with all the work he could desire.

His expertise was requested in Lucknow, Madras and Lahore, even as far south as Bombay, while smaller branch lines awaited his jurisdiction. He stood at the pinnacle of his profession as a railway engineer. Modestly he did not accept all the praise that came his way, but insisted that all those who had shared the work with him should also have some of the credit, particularly the native artisans. Those whose work was in the more dangerous localities were paid danger money, those injured were recompensed for their time lost from work, and men who were totally incapacitated were awarded a pension. But although Reginald's own position now seemed secure, the situation in his home was deteriorating.

Less than 12 months after the birth of her last child, Alexandra was once again pregnant, and once more she fell into a state of depression. Life in Cooch Behar held no joys for her now, and her marriage was heading for disaster. Her only happiness was in her children, and her visits to her parents' home. Here she took up her existence almost as though she was a girl again, enjoying the tennis parties and dances in the company of her sister. She also made the long journey to Simla to be presented to the Viceroy, looking, it was said, as radiant as a young girl again. Although she was by now the mother of Rex and four daughters, she appeared as lovely as ever. She stayed at Simla on three occasions for the summer season, taking her daughters with her, and Rex as well on at least one of these visits. There Rex had his only taste of schooling in India when he was obliged to attend with his younger sisters a kindergarten run by two English ladies, the Misses Birrell, in the grounds of the Viceregal residence which adjoined the English College at Simla.

Alexandra's visits to Darjeeling tended to grow longer and she took her four daughters with her, but left Rex behind with his father. The boy did not like life in Darjeeling where he said 'Nothing exciting ever happened', but plenty happened in and around Cooch Behar, and the railway.

In 1898, the rainy season had been more prolonged and catastrophic than usual. The plains were awash, the rivers swollen, the Torsa had broken its banks in several places, and the lines were under water on the lower levels. Reginald and his men worked around the clock to keep the trains running, then late one night the Kalua Bridge was threatened. Heavy tree trunks groaned and ground against the supports. The corpses of drowned cattle and other animals swept down from the upper reaches, their swollen bodies turning and rolling in the thick white foam which swirled like dingy soap suds through the piers.

Reginald drove down to the east bank of the river where a crowd of his men had gathered. Storm lanterns glimmered fitfully, and by their light it was seen that the up train must be halted before it reached the doomed bridge. Far away down the valley through the wind and driving rain a whistle was heard, and a red plume of smokey flame shone like a steaming torch from the smoke stack of the approaching engine. It was still a good way down the valley, and apparently unaware of the danger.

The telegraph lines having fallen during the nights' storm, it was not possible to get a message through to the last halt so Reginald, who had driven down to the bridge in his trap shouted to his syce to unhitch the horse, and stripping off his coat and boots jumped onto its back and disappeared into the darkness at full gallop. He knew that there was a ford about a mile away. Having located it, he got off the horse and left it by the bank. He waded out cautiously into the torrent. In no time he lost his foothold, and was swept off his feet. He struck out for the far side though forced to allow the current to carry him down stream, and trusting to an eddy was drawn over towards the bank. He dragged himself out and set off, until he found himself on the railway track near to the deserted signal box. He was only just in time: as the warning whistle sounded, and the train slowly serpented into sight, he pulled the signal lever to STOP. Later that night the bridge did give way, and no trains could get through until the waters subsided and the damage was repaired. Rex was greatly thrilled when he learnt of his father's adventure and courage.

On his seventh birthday Rex was given a pony of his own, and was allowed to ride out with his father on the tours of inspection up and down the line. It was a wonderful life for a boy. He rode on the footplates of the service engines, and learnt all the controls, although he was not allowed to use them; but he pulled the whistle cord, and threw logs into the firebox until he was smothered with smuts and wood ash. Reginald piloted them both down the river on a raft, manoeuvring the shallow rapids, and took him on expeditions climbing the second slopes of the nearby mountain ranges. Rex rode the work elephants, and learnt elephant language from the mahouts.

One never to be forgotten night, he went with his father to a village where a man-eating tiger had killed a woman and carried away her child. The terrified villagers had sent a message to Sahib Warneford asking him to come out and rid them of this terror. A tree platform had been built, and Reginald, a loader, and Rex climbed up and hid themselves there at dusk and waited for the tiger to make an appearance. A yellow moon came up from behind the hills, and lit the open patch of ground below the tree. Occasionally the silence was broken by the harsh cry of a night bird, and the irregular bleat of the goat which was tied to a stake to lure the tiger within reach of the guns. Through the undergrowth it suddenly appeared, its golden and ebony-striped skin clearly visible in the bright moonlight. Rex, trembling with excitement as he waited for his father to take aim, found himself wishing that the beautiful beast did not have to be killed. The tiger padded forward, then stopped and sniffed the air. It threw its head back, uttered a fearful roar, and an answering roar echoed from deeper in the dark jungle — the tiger's mate was on her way to join in the feast.

The unhappy goat continued to bleat helplessly, and pulled ineffectually on the rope. The first great animal stood perfectly still. Reginald brought the sights of his gun to bear until the tiger's magnificent head was full between them. He drew the trigger back, released it, there was a flash, a sharp report — the tiger leapt its full length straight into the air, and fell dead. Rex was stunned, shocked by the drama of the sudden death so close to him. The sight of this great creature lying lifeless below the tree suddenly brought unwilling tears to his eyes. Not so the villagers who seemed to appear from nowhere, firing their old-fashioned rifles wildly, loaded with bits of glass, nails, and home-made bullets, demonstrating their gratitude for having been relieved of the menace of the marauding tiger.

A year later Rex was given his first gun, a present from the Rajah of Cooch Behar. It was small, beautifully chased, with silver on its dark polished stock. Alexandra was furious with this dangerous gift and wanted to confiscate it, but Reginald insisted that Rex should be allowed to keep it, and only handle it under his own strict supervision. Alexandra continued to disapprove more and more of Reginald's ideas of bringing up their son but Rex, undisturbed by these arguments, followed his father like a puppy, and lived all the hours of daylight with him wherever they went.

He had no conventional schooling: his father taught him the law of the jungle; to read the moon and stars across the wide Indian night skies; to be able to study cloud formations, read their benevolent messages, and their ominous threats. Rex learned to speak and understand the native dialects, as his father had done as a child on the Andaman Islands. Of all of this Alexandra and her family disapproved. She was jealous of her husband's influence on Rex, but her protests fell on deaf ears, so she confined her attentions to her four daughters, these differences widening the rift in this now unhappy marriage.

Reginald seemed unaware of the threat. He was now often working away from home, as the Cooch Behar Railway had opened a second extension, with through booking for both passengers and goods traffic, for foreign railways. From the first of January, 1899, another extension was built to Kholtaon, the frontier of the Cooch Behar State, and over the mountain passes below the snows of Bhutan and on to the tea gardens of Darjeeling.

In the autumn of 1899, Alexandra left Reginald for ever. There were to be no reconciliations this time. One day she ordered her boxes to be packed, gathered her daughters, and leaving no message told the syce to drive to the station. Everyone in the bungalow was sent to search for Rex but, fearful of losing her train, Alexandra left without him. That evening when his father returned to the silent empty rooms he found Rex sitting in the darkness waiting for him.

For a few days there was no news from Darjeeling, and Alexandra's departure was hardly mentioned. After all she had left them before, sometimes for quite long periods, and returned. Neither Rex nor his father realised how bitter she had become. This time she would never come back. She would send for Rex, but Reginald would never see or speak with her again.

3

Goodbye India

Alexandra had no intention of leaving Rex for long at Cooch Behar. Her brother and Captain Campbell drove up to the bungalow and, after a short chilling interview with Reginald, took a defiant and miserable Rex back to Darjeeling. Reginald was left completely alone. Everything to do with his marriage was to be wiped out.

At Darjeeling, though there was nothing but memories of the last ten years, his name was forbidden to be mentioned. It is hard to understand how love could turn into such cruel hatred. Reginald could not bring himself to believe that his wife would never allow him to see his children again. The loss of Rex hit him the hardest. What were they telling the boy? How would they answer his questions? How could a child understand?

Reginald descended into such grief and despair that even his closest friends could not comfort him, and he sought oblivion in drinking himself unconscious night after night. Eventually his drinking and moods lost him one job after another. One day Cooch Behar knew him no more. He tossed a few belongings into a suitcase, went to the stables and shot Rex's pony dead rather than leave it to be sold in the bazaars; a common fate of many horses and ponies when their European owners moved away.

For nearly one year nothing was heard of Reginald. Then Alexandra received a cheque from a firm of auctioneers, being the total sum from the sale of the contents of the bungalow at Cooch Behar, asking that it should be kept in trust for Rex. Finally, in the autumn of 1900, an Indian lawyer friend of Reginald Warneford received a communication from the superintendent of a hospital in Bombay, stating that Reginald had been picked up unconscious in a street and died a short time after he had been admitted to the hospital. His identity had been established by papers that he was carrying on him at the time. A small book of poems held a letter to his friend asking that, in the event of his death, the book might be delivered to his son. Addresses were enclosed, so this last wish was faithfully carried out.

Alexandra did not mourn for Reginald, and her family were frankly relieved that with his death there was no chance of ever seeing him again. But Rex was inconsolable for many long days and nights. To make it worse he had to conceal his grief, as there was no one who could share it with him. He treasured the book of poems. His father had written on the flyleaf some lines of verse which he must somehow have felt would one day have a meaning for his son.

> '*... I see afar*
> *O'ersailing the blue cragginess, a car*
> *And steeds with streamy manes — the charioteer*
> *Looks out upon the winds with glorious fear:*
> *And now the numerous tramplings quiver lightly*
> *Along a huge cloud's ridge; and now with sprightly*
> *Wheel downward come they into fresher skies,*
> *Tipt round with silver from the sun's bright eyes.*
>
> . . . .
>
> *The visions all are fled — the car is fled*
> *Into the light of heaven, and in their stead*
> *A sense of real things comes doubly strong,*
> *. . . . . . '*

Sleep and Poetry, Keats 1817

Keat's words, and their choice by his father, kindled in Rex's mind the glories of the limitless sky that they had so often watched together. But his childhood dreams were over; from now on Rex knew he had to sink or swim by his own determination. He gave up all hope of finding someone who would ever understand him as his father had done.

Alexandra tried to regain his confidence, but he had become wary of her, and knew that it was she who had caused this cataclysm in his young life. The sister who had the most affection for him was Jeanne, the second daughter. The elder, Gladys, was fast becoming a young lady and enjoyed parties (which he detested) and the other two, Dorothy and Violet, were far too young to take much notice of the change in their situation. But Rex still loved his mother in spite of everything. He admired her tremendously, and always thought of her as 'Pretty Mama.'

There was a lot of sympathy for the beautiful young widow in Darjeeling. Rex had always been dazzled by her lovely trailing flounced dresses, her jewels, and her scent. Now in her widow's weeds she was more appealing than ever. Widowhood had lent her a frail exquisite aura. Would-be admirers followed her progress with adoring eyes as she drove to the English church on Sundays, accompanied by her pretty daughters in white dresses, large hats, and black ribbons: Rex absolved himself from church when he got the chance.

Although she was only 27 years old at the time of Reginald's death, Alexandra vowed that she would never marry again. However 12 months later she discarded her mourning, and was married, looking as pretty as a picture in a bewitching hat and a dress of white muslin, with a blue sash around her still 18-inch waist.

Her new husband was Captain M P Corkery, an Irishman, who had always been in love with her, and remained so during a long marriage in which he survived her by only a few years.

Captain Corkery tried to do his best to be a father to the young and spirited family he had inherited. Dorothy and Violet remember him to this day with affection, but the three older ones never took him to their hearts. Rex could not get on with him and showed the most rebellion; he began as he meant to go on and there was no way of bringing him to heel. No-one was ever going to take the place of his late father, and in spite of pleadings from Alexandra he refused to alter his attitude. Sullen silences developed into open revolt. The situation became so strained that at last it was not possible for the two to exist peaceably under the same roof. He was sent to stay with his grandparents until it was decided what could be done with him.

Finally a family conference was called. Captain Campbell took the seat of honour as 'judge', and very severe he looked; other members of the family, including Captain Corkery, formed the jury. Rex was banished to his bedroom: he was not present at his 'trial', nor was he allowed to make any contribution towards his 'defence'. The verdict was unanimous: it was high time he was sent to England for his education. That suggestion filled the bill very satisfactorily, for the family anyway, and in the end it was not to turn out too badly for Rex either.

It was decided that the best person to approach concerning his future was his own grandfather, Tom Lewis Warneford. One of the enemy camp indeed, but what better choice was there? He could safely be relied upon not to shirk any of the responsibilities of Rex's rehabilitation. Thus could the task be safely taken off the Campbell and Corkery shoulders. Cables shuttled to and fro between the Rectory in Satley, and the Campbell bungalow in Darjeeling.

Rex, meanwhile, was in an agony of apprehension as to what was going to happen to him. He was not told very much. In less than a month after negotiations had begun, his few possessions were packed into a small tin trunk and little case with the necessities for the voyage. He was taken down to Calcutta by his Uncle Campbell, who was rather sympathetic towards the small boy being sent all alone on such a long voyage, to meet the grandfather whom he had never seen.

There had been a tearful farewell from Alexandra, whose conscience pricked her at the last moments of parting, when she clung to the slight little body who nearly had to be torn away from her: but there was a shared sense of relief when the last goodbyes were over and they were able to take up life again, without the ever-present embarrassment of the unhappy and rebellious Rex.

All alone, on board the big P&O steamer, Rex stood at the stern watching the high buildings, the docks and the busy river Hooghly traffic fade away into the mist as the ship made its way into the Bay of Bengal. He turned away as darkness hid the shores of India, and made his way to the second-class accommodation which had been reserved for him. He was under the charge of the purser, who did his best to make life on board interesting; and on the whole Rex did enjoy the trip. He was quite sorry to say goodbye to the passengers and the ship's company who had made him feel at home.

When the steamer berthed at Tilbury, a small elderly clergyman came up the gangway to claim the grandson who was to do much to make up for the tragedy of his own son Reginald. Now out of the far East, which grandfather Tom had known for so many years, came Rex like a lost child, his own flesh and blood, to bring new life to the old parson. What an experience for them both.

The Rev Thomas Lewis Warneford

4

School Days

It was certainly a momentous meeting for grandfather and grandson, and it was a great relief for Tom Warneford to learn that the boy's character was so very different from the description hinted at by his in-laws. Rex very quickly realized that his grandfather was a wonderful and considerate person, who liked to listen to the stories of the railway his father had built, and the life he had enjoyed before everything at Cooch Behar was broken up.

At Satley Rectory where Rex soon settled down, he met his step-grandmother whom he thought must be very young, and her baby daughter Katharine. Katharine's mother was Tom's second wife, and they had been married in Ealing on July 16th, 1900. Her little girl was born at Satley on July 27th, 1902. She was a baby when Rex came to live at the Rectory, and he was just 11 years old. He spent a very happy Christmas at Satley.

Soon after his arrival his grandfather asked if he would like to sing in the choir. He had never sung in public before but with the encouragement of his step-grandmother, who played the organ, he said he would 'have a go'. He had a true, clear voice and came to enjoy the church services. He soon made friends with the other boys who sang in the choir, and they introduced him to many sports and games, when the snow came and cut off the village from the rest of civilisation. Rex was not a stranger to snow; he had seen plenty of it on the mountain slopes near Cooch Behar, but snow in England was different. It came very suddenly in the night after a storm. Rex woke to find drifts piled high against the walls and doors of the houses. The big stone rectory stood deep in it, and Rex was set to work to shovel a clear pathway to the church door so that the rector could take the services. During that winter milk came from the nearby farm on a sled, as did all other commodities that were needed to supplement the Rectory store cupboards.

The holidays passed far too quickly, and when January 1903 came in with bitter winds and driving sleet, Rex knew that at the beginning of the new term he was to be sent away to school. He would have liked to stay at Satley, and go to the village school, but Tom would have none of that. His grandson was to be properly equipped to make his way in the world, and that meant going to a public school. Tom's choice fell upon the King Edward VI school at Stratford-upon-Avon for several reasons: it did not have many boarders, which made the atmosphere more homely; and the new headmaster was a personal friend. All the headmasters, from the first, William Smart in 1553, to the present day, brought something to add to the exceptional traditions of the famous school, where it has been said that Shakespeare was a pupil. Rex was enrolled as a choral scholar owing to the pleasant qualities of his voice and, contrary to his expectations, he was very happy during the short period he remained there.

He spent his holidays at Satley Rectory. Tom organised many interesting expeditions, some quite near home, driving the fat pony along white dusty roads still innocent of macadam. By train they visited the nearby coalfields, and the fine cathedral of Durham, where Tom was one of the sub-chanters.

Rex loved to explore the western part of the county, the barren moors, deep wooded dales, and the clear peaty streams crossed by pack horse bridges. On these lonely roads, traffic consisted of farm wagons, and an occasional carrier's cart, travelling from village to village with assorted merchandise for the isolated farmers' wives and country folk, who hardly saw a town from one year's end to another. Satley was not so cut off, but it had only one village street, a scatter of outlying farms, and an inn known as the Punch Bowl.

On retirement from his chaplaincy in India Tom had been given the living through the good offices of his great friend General Sir Donald Stewart who, after a period of acting as governor to the Chelsea Hospital, had died in Algiers early in 1901. His body had been brought back to England on a destroyer, and buried with full military honours in Brompton cemetery. Tom felt the loss of his friend deeply, for they had served together for many years in the Indian Army. He went south to attend the funeral, and when there made arrangements that when he died he should be buried as near General Stewart as was possible.

Rex's arrival at the Rectory made a great difference to the old man, who enjoyed reminiscing about his own long time in the east, with the dangers and adventures during the great march to Kabul. Rex never tired of listening to these stories about the skirmishes with the wild Northern Frontier tribesmen on their sure-footed ponies, brandishing their curved swords. He was allowed to hold Tom's famous old sword, and to gaze at the Medal of Ahmed Khel in its leather case. He always remembered his grandfather's words on the subject of medals. 'Medals are very nice to have, but they are not the be-all and end-all of battles. What counts most is to know how you behaved when in a tight corner, not only in the excitement of an attack, but in adversity and difficulties met in your daily life, when things seem to go wrong, and it is hard to keep going and show a cheerful face.'

Tom became very fond of Rex, who, he often said, was 'the blessing of his old age.' He was very anxious that the boy should have a good start, and that Fate would treat him more generously than it had his father. He hoped he would be able to live a good life and solve the problems which had so far eluded him. Tom worried that when he was gone there would be no-one who would be able to solve them, as he knew that Rex would not find it easy to place any confidence in strangers. But for the time being all was set fair, and Rex felt that given a chance he would be able to fend for himself when out in the World.

At Stratford-upon-Avon he was able to prove this, to the great satisfaction of his grandfather. He found that although he was behind other boys in such subjects as History, Latin and Greek, he excelled at anything he could do with his hands, such as carpentry, physics, engineering, and, surprisingly, mathematics. The masters

Rex at Stratford-upon-Avon

liked him but found him decidedly 'individualistic'. The boys thought him 'a character'. There were a good many encounters, but he came out of them well, and showed himself capable of looking after himself in a scrimmage. He was not a particularly enthusiastic games man, and not at all keen on the football matches played on the wet cold fields on the far side of the river during the winter afternoons. Nor did he fancy fielding under a hot sun for a ball which seldom came his way. He preferred to go for long walks on his own, and, when he got the chance, to go down to the station and goods yards to study the locomotives and rolling stock which he compared with those he knew so well in India. At one time Tom thought it might be a wise thing to apprentice the boy to the locomotive works at Crewe, where a Warneford cousin was superintendent; but he never got round to it. This cousin, Walter Warneford, had a brilliant only son, W K F G Warneford, who was to lose his life on July 14th, 1919 when his airship *NS11* was lost in a thunderstorm off Sheringham.

During 1904 grandfather Tom was taken seriously ill, and had to relinquish his living at Satley. He went to live with his daughter Maude Nightingale at Ealing, which was a setback for Rex, who had just begun to feel that he had found security with his grandfather at Satley. The Nightingales lived in a small semi-detached house with their two children, Meta and Roger, and had little room for the entire new family, so Tom's wife with baby Katharine moved into lodgings a few doors up the road from her sick husband.

Ealing was a poor substitute for the wide moors of County Durham; with its rows of red brick semi-detached houses, each one set in a small plot of garden, enclosed by a wrought iron railing. The plate glass windows of the shops on the Broadway had no attraction for him, after the little shop at Satley, which sold twisted barley

29

sugar sticks and huge black and white humbugs. There were trams in Ealing, swaying and clanging on their shallow lines: there had been trams in Calcutta, but Rex had never ridden on one; they could not hold a candle to a real steam locomotive.

Early in 1900 the first few motor cars had begun to make an appearance in the streets; horse cabs plied for hire, and stood in rows outside the station waiting for a fare. The horses which drew them had their bits taken out at lunch time, and nosebags hung on their heads. Troops of ubiquitous sparrows hopped beside them, picking up the grain which dropped from their mouths. Tradespeople still delivered their goods to the back door by horse and cart. The butcher in his blue and white striped apron drove a smart high-stepping cob, which fairly rattled along between calls. The milkman drove a much slower pony which walked sedately, and stopped at every gate putting its feet up on the curb, while a maid came out with a jug, and the milk was dipped from a brass-bound gleaming churn — a pint at a time with a few extra dips for good measure. The greengrocer hawked his wares along the tree-lined avenues on a flat cart pulled by a little aged pony, calling out 'Nice fresh greens today, apples a penny a pound.'

But in spite of all these diversions Rex was not happy. After the large north country rectory, the red brick house at Ealing seemed very cramped, and there were no spare rooms where he could hide away and read a book in peace. Mr and Mrs Nightingale were very kind, but he did not get on very well with Meta and Roger. He felt he was among strangers again, and became wary and withdrawn. Grandfather Tom was slipping away from life. Since he had left Satley he seemed to have lost the will to live, and Rex was left to his own devices. Aunt Maude was glad when he was out of the house; he only moped around and she could not find anything indoors to keep him interested, so she gave him some money and sent him off to see places of 'educational value'.

Hampton Court was his favourite. He enjoyed finding his way through the maze, and delighted in decoying lost ones into worse muddles than when he first encountered them. When he was tired of the maze, he sat by the riverside munching his sandwiches, contemplating the river steamers, and intrepid pleasure-seekers energetically rowing skiffs in spite of the wintry spring weather. He rode miles on the top of horse buses, his feet tucked under a tarpaulin apron, and when his money ran out, walked back to Ealing late in the dark evenings when the gas lamps made pools of light along the barren pavements. No-one bothered to ask where he had been.

Grandfather Tom, drifting into his last sleep, no longer knew the time of day. He lay in a quiet backwater of existence where sleep is but the harbinger of death. He still knew Rex when he tiptoed to the bedside, but very little else concerning him. The summer term of 1904 had been Rex's last at Stratford-upon-Avon: there were no more funds to spend on his education. He would have no part in making plans, discussing the cricket eleven, or the launching of the new boat on the river. The sense of isolation which he had hoped had left him, came back in all intensity, and robbed him of sleep. He woke several times in a night, turning and twisting to solve the puzzle of his future. He was to be, so he was told by Uncle Nightingale, sent back to India and apprenticed to the British India Steam Navigation Company.

5

To the Pacific and the Orient

On January 11th 1905 Rex began his new life by working his passage out to Calcutta as an apprentice on the *SS Somali*, a liner of the Peninsular & Oriental Steam Navigation Company (now P&O-Orient Lines), the parent company of the British India Steam Navigation Company which he was to join.

The saddest part of his leave-taking was saying goodbye to Grandfather Tom whom he felt he would never see again. Then he dutifully said his farewells to Aunt Maude and his two young cousins; he was sure they would not be very sorry to see him go. The cab was at the door: his small trunk, the same one that had accompanied him on his last P&O voyage from India, was heaved up onto the roof. Rex hesitated for a moment, looking up to Grandfather Tom's bedroom window, hoping to catch a glimpse of his kind old face, but there was no sign of him.

Uncle Nightingale gave him a little push into the musty-smelling interior of the cab, and stepped in beside him. They took the train at Ealing for London and reached Tilbury where the *SS Somali* lay at the dockside. It was bitterly cold: a sprinkling of snow whitened the roofs of the sheds and the superstructure of ships on the river. Masts and tall cranes were etched black against the grey leaden sky. The Lascar sailors preparing the ship for departure looked wizened and frozen in their thin clothes.

Uncle Nightingale led Rex up the gangway and introduced him to the ship's purser who stood at the rail: Rex's prospects were explained to him before bells began to ring all over the decks, warning people who were seeing off their friends and relations that it was time to go. Uncle Nightingale, eager to get away and leave his young nephew to his fate, gave Rex a tip, shook his hand, clattered down the gangway and just disappeared. Rex, standing alone, waved to a receding back view of his uncle and turned away feeling himself quite abandoned.

He walked forward rather at a loss; even the purser had found more important work to do than play nurse to a small boy who would soon have to find his place on board for himself. Suddenly he heard a cheery voice, and towering above him was an enormous black cook, clad in white jacket and trousers, who laid a vast hand across Rex's shoulders and said that he had been sent topsides to look for him. Rex followed in the wide wake of his mentor through polished mahogany and teakwood corridors, down shining brass-railed companionways, into the galleys of the ship.

The galleys were already full of steam as groups of busy cooks were preparing the first evening meal for the passengers, while stewards kept dashing through the

The P&O liner 'Somali'

pantry swing-doors shouting orders. The noise was cacophonous. In the midst of the bustle Rex was introduced to a ginger-haired lad who was stacking empty tea-trays, and on being told to help him soon found himself so busy that he had no time to feel lost. He filled milk jugs and set the trays under the critical eyes of the older boy who was obviously an old hand at the job. His name was Alf, as Rex found out when he plucked up the courage to ask; he was a true cockney, born near the docks. This was his second trip, and he seemed to Rex to be very sure of himself indeed. All around appeared chaotic, but Alf assured him that things would settle down to a pretty steady routine as soon as they were at sea.

There were several other apprentices aboard and Rex soon came to know them. They were all due to join other ships in different capacities later after having started at the bottom, learning to make themselves useful everywhere and to obey orders without question. They wore the uniform of the company, and were under the eagle eye of the Chief Steward and the first-class smoking room Steward, who gave them their orders at the morning inspection parade: woe betide any boy whose hair was untidy, hands, nails or ears dirty, or whose shoes and buttons were not polished then. Their work included arranging daily papers and periodicals in the first class lounges and smoking rooms, running messages, delivering telegrams, emptying ashtrays, serving drinks, buying stamps, posting letters, finding lost children, and a hundred usual and unusual tasks which kept them on their feet from dawn until late in the evening. They had always to be willing, polite, patient, clean and friendly without being familiar.

The *SS Somali* was one of the company's newer ships, having been built at

Greenock in 1901, and she was also one of their larger vessels, 450 feet long, 52 feet in the beam and 34 feet deep in the hold. She had two masts, fore and aft schooner-rigged, and an elliptical stern. Two sets of triple-expansion engines, direct acting with two boilers of 170 pounds pressure, gave her an overall speed of 14 knots.

At high water she was moved out into mid-stream by three twin-funnelled tugs which accompanied her to Gravesend. At the river mouth she left them and proceeded under her own steam to the Nore where she stopped to pick up mails and newspapers and to drop the pilot. Rex had managed to take a few minutes off duty to give him a postcard to send to Grandfather Tom when he returned to shore in the waiting cutter.

As the *Somali* steamed down the Channel Rex was kept busy until the first-class passengers had finished dining and dispersed to their various lounges for after-dinner drinks and coffee. Then at last the boys had a 'stand easy', and before going to their bunks went on deck to see the Eddystone lighthouse off Plymouth flashing its warning beam across the shipping lanes, and the twinkling lights of the south coast towns diminishing before being swallowed up in darkness.

Early next morning Rex and Alf were on duty again laying tables for breakfast, a meal to which not many were expected to turn up, since, once off Ushant, the steamer's bow began to rise and fall considerably as she met the long ocean swell rolling eastward from the Atlantic. Less-seasoned passengers soon found the motion too much for them, and retired to lie down, shut their eyes, and endure. Many of the ladies in particular battened themselves down in their stuffy cabins where they were ministered to by patient stewardesses amid a chaos of steamer trunks, plaid rugs and basins, as the *SS Somali* pitched and rolled across the Bay of Biscay.

Swept by the winter gales, the bay was formidable, and the dining saloons did indeed remain deserted except for a few hardy souls, and on the long tables reduced numbers of plates and glasses were kept from sliding to the floor by the guards, called fiddles, fixed along the edges, while the paraffin lamps tilted and smoked in their gimbals above. Life on board passenger ships at the beginning of the century was different in many ways from that of today's luxury cruises in huge, modern, oil-powered liners. It was a more spartan existence for passengers and crew alike, but even so Rex was always a good sailor, and slept soundly at the end of his day's work.

While they were crossing the Bay of Biscay, however, there was not so much for him to do in the saloons and lounges, so he was allowed to explore the inner workings of the ship. He scrambled down steep steel ladders to the engine room, where the gleaming pistons revolved slowly; and even further down he watched the Indian greasers with their long-nosed oil cans crawling on their stomachs to grease the great propeller shafts turning smoothly, almost silently, in their bearings, by the dim light of oil lamps.

During the bad weather storm sails had been rigged to keep the ship's head steady as she ploughed her way across the raging bay; but when she reached calmer waters the sails were struck and the passengers began to reappear on the deck, to sit like pale shadows of their former selves on the sunnier side of the ship. Once again the boys found themselves busy ministering to their wants.

At Gibraltar the passengers left the ship in droves, fleeing from the clouds of coal-dust which filled the air as baskets of coal were carried up the side and tipped into the ship's bunkers. Dust seeped into every nook and cranny, and there was a lot of cleaning to be done as soon as coaling was completed. The boys, who had to help in this, were black before all was shipshape again. It was not a job which anyone enjoyed.

Steamers at that time burnt great quantities of solid fuel, and there were coaling stations all along the routes they travelled. For the *Somali* these included Malta, Port Said, Colombo and Bombay. At Malta, while the lighters came out from the port and tied up alongside for the coaling routine to be resumed, there were also fruit, lace and bird sellers swarming round in their small boats, shouting prices and showing their wares.

Through increasing heat, the ship approached Port Said and in the Suez Canal she passed her sister ship, the *SS Victoria* homeward bound, so closely that the two ships seemed to touch. Passengers crowded to the rails, shouted messages, and threw letters and small parcels to be sent on at the end of each voyage.

By now people aboard had settled into various cliques: the military and their wives travelling back to their stations after leave usually kept together, as did the tea and rubber planters bound for Ceylon and Assam. One evening Rex overheard the name Darjeeling spoken by a man from one of these groups while playing cards. The name sent cold shivers down his spine and henceforth he avoided the tables where they played their after-dinner game.

Many of the women, especially the motherly kind, were curious about the boy. He was always so pleasant, and the harassed Mamas and Nannies found him very obliging in helping with their fractious charges. They discussed his good looks shamefully in his presence, which made him blush to the roots of his hair, and they tried to inveigle him into telling them about his family and background: but he shut up like a clam and invented some excuse to escape politely from his interrogators. The most they got out of his friend Alf was that Rex was 'an Orfan', and they had to leave it at that, for Rex would not be induced to discuss his father or his 'pretty Mama' with anybody.

As the ship progressed further into the Indian Ocean the heat hung over her like a scorching blanket. The sky burned and there was not a ripple or a cool breeze. Now the *Somali*, her black plume of smoke trailing astern, was followed by shoals of flying fish, and by hungry sharks diving and snapping at the ship's garbage as it was tipped out of the chutes. They turned their white bellies upwards, vicious small eyes glinting with greed as they swallowed voraciously, then fell away, gorged, into the churning wake, to reappear later as hungry as ever.

Because of the heat, the male passengers pulled their mattresses out onto the decks at night, while their womenfolk modestly remained in their suffocating cabins, fanning themselves with the large dried palm leaves distributed at the dining tables by the generosity of the P&O company. There was no air-conditioning on board in those days, and the lazy punkahs did little to alleviate the discomfort of the public saloons and nothing to cool the cabins. At dawn the Lascars came with their buckets of white sand and hard brushes to scrub and wash down the decks, and late sleepers were obliged to relinquish their cool places and go below to the stifling cabins.

On the indigo star-studded nights, the stays of the awnings over the upper decks were festooned with fairy lights; the band played, and when the passengers had finished their dinner they slowly wended their way in little groups, some to dance, others to lean over the ship's rail and watch the phosphorescent wake twisting and turning. The smoking room portholes were kept wide open to the night air, and the heavy scent of cheroots and brandy assailed Rex's nose as he passed by on an errand, reminding him of his father smoking cigars back home in the bungalow at Cooch Behar. The only cool place on board was the ship's refrigerator, an icy black store room stocked with carcasses of meat, ducks, chickens, game and salmon, frozen to the consistency of stone, hanging and lying amid blocks of ice.

Each Sunday morning the Captain read the prayers at divine service in the lounge of the long first-class saloon, while down in the stoke-hole the seedie boys flung coal endlessly into the rows of furnaces under the two huge cylindrical boilers. At Bombay the ship coaled again, and many of her passengers disembarked. Others came aboard, and she steamed on south to Colombo; then, after once more filling her insatiable bunkers, she started on the last lap of her voyage, 700 sea miles to Calcutta.

There Rex left her, and was met by two old friends of Grandfather Tom with whom he stayed until he took up his next appointment with the P&O. He had no relations living in India: Captain Campbell, now retired, was living in Ireland; 'pretty Mama', Captain Corkery, and his four sisters were all at home in England.

He was anxious to start the next stage of his new life as soon as possible and the day after his disembarkation from the *Somali* found him at the downtown office of the British India Steam Navigation Company in Calcutta for an interview. Rex was ushered into a large room whose walls and bookcases were cluttered with photographs and models in glass cases of many famous vessels, past and present, of the P&O Company. The large plate glass windows looked over the harbour and river traffic of the Hooghly.

The personnel manager regarded Rex with interest, as he knew part of the boy's background: this was the son of Reginald Warneford who had undertaken and succeeded in the difficult task of building the Cooch Behar railway. The interview was a success and Rex was apprenticed on board the mail boat *Ekma* which operated between Calcutta and Rangoon. This craft carried cargo and two classes of passengers, 50 first-class and 36 second. She also carried unberthed passengers who crowded her decks laden with all their worldly possessions in shapeless bundles and corded boxes, livestock being crammed on board in whatever space remained.

Shortly before Christmas 1905 Rex received news of the death of Grandfather Tom. Although he had known when he left London in January that year he would never see the old man again, the actual knowledge that he had died came as a great shock. Grandfather Tom was the only one who had led him out of his Slough of Despond and put his feet on the right path, and his wise counsels were never forgotten. He had been and always was Rex's guiding light. When he had died at the drab little house in Ealing on July 16th he was buried as he wished, near to the grave of his old friend Sir Donald Stewart in Brompton cemetery, London.

Altogether Rex was to spend nearly eight years with the British India Steam Navigation Company. He sailed in different capacities on 14 of their ships, starting as an unpaid apprentice, all found, which included expenses, full board and living accommodation; until eventually, on January 10th 1911 he was promoted to Fourth Officer, which brought a small stipend.

The ships he served in, carrying passengers and cargo, ran on different routes along the Indian and Malayan coasts. They had names as musical to the ear as their ports of call: the *Lhasa,* of the Bombay and Karachi Mail Service; the *Lalpoora, Lama* and *Lindula* were four of the larger ones. The little cargo vessels *Dwarka, Vadala* and the *Itola,* which was nearly sunk in a typhoon, carried immigrants and pilgrims from Madras and Bombay to Mecca.

These pilgrim boats were the worst: small and loaded to the gunwales. Built with shallow draught for trading between villages on the rivers, they also carried bales of cotton, sacks of rice and maize, live cattle and bales of cloth. The smell on board was indescribable; pilgrims accompanied by their goats and chickens slept packed like sardines amid a clutter of cooking pots and bedding rolls. Some of them died on the journey; some were born; and some, who had never been to sea in their lives, panicked as soon as they were out of harbour, and tried to throw themselves overboard. Smuggling of opium and other drugs was rife. Customs officers came out in their steam pinnaces at the various ports of call and endeavoured to interrogate the heaps of humanity on board, mostly with small success.

From the Gulf of Aden to Rangoon, Sumatra and Singapore; across the Indian Ocean, the Bay of Bengal; to the China Sea and along the Chinese coastline to Shanghai and Hong Kong, there were few harbours east of Suez that Rex had not visited at one time or another during his duties on these ships. At a time when most English boys of his age were still at their schools he had lived a fair slice of life in these far-away colourful places, with shipmates who were men of many races and castes, a tough lot who lived by the law of the jungle. Words they had little use for, except those necessary to keep the boats sailing. They were always ready to settle an argument in the only way they knew, with their fists or their knives.

Rex learned to live with them, and took his share of the rough-housing with good humour. His quick brain got him out of many a tight corner, and his superior officers put a considerable amount of trust in him, as revealed by an occasion when he was on night watch single-handed, and managed to stave off a boat-load of Chinese bent on sneaking a free passage, without any bloodshed.

He soon grew accustomed to the typhoons which tore across the seas with scant warning, sending the little steamers almost onto their beam-ends in a welter of tossing water and blinding rain. He wandered round the docksides of the seaports, looking in at the gambling halls, drinking houses and opium dens, and made good friends with the girls at the tea-houses. He sent the crew of one of his ships into paroxysms of laughter by describing how he took tea with one of the most notorious 'ladies of joy' in Shanghai, and managed to emerge from all this none the worse but a good deal wiser. His acquaintances included an assortment of the human flotsam and jetsam of all the many places where his boat put in to discharge cargo: Chinese drug traffickers, pirates, harbour police, and fishermen and their families who lived on the lateen-sailed junks that often carried contrabrand from Shanghai to Macao. The danger, the squalor, the hardships did him no harm at all, but made a better man of him. He savoured to the full his uninhibited existence and enjoyed every minute of it. Life could never be quite so good again.

Rex on board ship with his terrier Vic

6

Hospital in Calcutta

While Rex was outward bound to Rangoon on the *SS Arangola* he was laid low with a severe attack of appendicitis. As the ship had been at sea only a few days, they put back, and Rex was taken off and sent to hospital at Calcutta. He was not a very placid patient. As soon as his operation was successfully completed and he was off the danger list, he drove the nurses to distraction with wild compliments in order to wheedle them into allowing him to get up. He also wanted to smoke, which was strictly forbidden as his stitches had not been taken out and smoke would make him cough.

One of his friends recalls the following story:

'I certainly did not dare to go against authority and smuggle him in packets of fags, but I later heard when I visited him how he got round the ban. That morning the orderlies came to Rex's bedside, lifted him onto a wheeled stretcher, and pushed him out of the ward to await his turn to go into the surgery to have his wound inspected by the surgeon. There had been no complications, but Rex had been warned that on no account was he to fool around during his convalescence.

In the corridor where he had been left, his eyes explored his surroundings: nothing of interest in sight: bare green walls with a darker dado, and a notice, NO SMOKING, in large letters. The orderlies came shuffling back pushing another stretcher which they placed alongside Rex. On it lay a rubicund cheerful individual. He looked at the notice, then at Rex.

"Poppycock!" he announced.

"My sentiments," replied Rex emphatically, "but what's the use, we haven't got any."

"I have," said the cheerful one, and produced a crumpled packet of gaspers from under his blanket and reached over with one for Rex. His neighbour was up to any eventuality, and from his other side he produced a box of matches.

By dint of pulling on the sides of each other's stretcher they got close enough to light up and lay blissfully puffing side by side. The orderlies returned and began to wheel Rex towards the theatre. He managed to conceal the cigarette, which was nearing its last gasp, underneath his blanket, and thought that he had put it out. The theatre sister approached, sniffing suspiciously:

"Can you smell burning?" she asked the surgeon. Suddenly she caught sight of a blue curly wisp of smoke coming from under Rex's blanket which was only too obviously about to burst into flames. All hell was let loose. A fire extinguisher was produced, orderlies were harangued; the surgeon, most put out at this happening, furiously went for Rex who was lying looking very smug among the charred remains of his blanket.

"What on earth do you think you are playing at?" he rebuked the harassed nurse, who seemed to think the question was directed at her. Outside in the corridor the instigator of the crime was lying peacefully on his back, the picture of innocence. There was no smell of charred blankets about him.

Rex's friends came to visit him that evening and were regaled with a spirited résumé of the morning's events.

"Now I am liable to be searched at all times of the day and night, especially after my visitors have left," complained Rex. "Most embarrassing for a fella. The ward sister is a dragon. She's still trying to find out where I got hold of that fag".'

The following story was printed in several newspapers round the world after his Zeppelin exploit, when any tales about him were news.

His friend recalls: 'One day when I visited him he was in one of his depressed moods. As soon as I came into the ward I saw he lay with his head down and there was no sign of his usual greeting. The nurse told me he had had a bit of trouble with the wound which would delay his release from hospital for a bit longer. Hence the depression. As I stood there beside his bed I was not sure whether to leave him to it and visit him another day, when he rolled over and looked at me.

"I am sick to death of lying here. Do something and get me out somehow."

He knew perfectly well that I could do nothing to get him out. They had not taken out all of the stitches, and I was scared even then that he was likely to fool around and do himself a serious injury, so I just walked out and left him, promising to come in again the next day. Then he was in a much better frame of mind; he had the news that the last stitches were to be taken out in the next few days, and then he assured me he would be as good as new: so ... would I arrange a party for him to have a celebration? It was to be held at a restaurant that he usually patronized when he came ashore from his travels. He left me to fix the menu, only stipulating that the food was to be interesting. Also I was to invite two pretty girls to make up a foursome. I must say that at this stage of his convalescence I was very loath to agree, but he was insistent, and, fearing one of his moods I thought the better course was to humour him and then try to get out of it later. What a forlorn hope! As I seemed to be agreeable to his plan he was all smiles at once.

"Look here!" he said, swung his legs over the side of the bed, stood up and pranced up and down the ward giving a fine illustration of Sister on her rounds. His performance was greatly appreciated by his audience, the other patients, who watched in delighted anticipation as they could see Sister approaching like a ship in full sail through the swing-doors. He was in for it again. He meekly got into bed winking at me behind the 'dragon's' back as he did so. I took my leave promptly as I saw Sister was shooting some pretty malevolent glances at me as she tucked him in, as though I was to blame for his outrageous behaviour.

I kept away for the next few days and when I did arrive Rex was in a rage as he had not been able to bring his plans any further forward without my assistance. It was in for a penny in for a pound as far as I could see, but a more unwilling accomplice could not have been found than my unhappy self. I decided to put some spanners in the works: as it transpired, to no avail.

I banged in No. 1 spanner: "How on earth are you going to get out of here?" I asked him hopefully. "You have not got any clothes."

I sat down on his bed. He caught hold of my arm in a surprisingly hard grip and whispered in my ear. It was worse than I had thought...

"Oh, no! I couldn't possibly fix that. I live in Calcutta. It's as much as my job is worth! I shall get the blame when you are safely out on the high seas."

Well, it was no use to try and put him off, so he got around me all right as even at the beginning I knew he would. He wanted me to get hold of a nurse's uniform — anything would do from a fancy dress shop — then smuggle it in to him on my next visit. I began to see, after some more explanations, that there might be something of a pretty good lark in his whole plan. After all, we were very young. So, very reluctantly, I did as he wished. We let the patients whose beds were on either side of his into the scheme. They, as they faced no danger to themselves, were more than enthusiastic, and agreed to everything that Rex suggested.

That evening after supper Rex put on the clothes which were, I must say, not the best of fits, and more suitable for the ample charms of Sister. The other conspirators encouraged him with pretty ribald remarks. He left the cap and cloak to the last, and, bundling them into his towel, set off for the bathroom, stuffing a blonde wig that I had procured for him into his dressing-gown pocket. The nurse on duty at her desk at the end of the ward did not take any notice of him. His two friends tidied up his bed after he had gone and put a dummy into it which they had made up of their own clothes to represent Rex lying asleep.

Meanwhile he had put the finishing touches to his disguise and emerged from the bathroom, keeping well to the back of the nurse who was still engrossed in her reports, and sidled through the swing-doors and out into the corridor. He met an orderly on the way out, to whom he addressed a cheerful 'good evening'. Gaining confidence he walked boldly out of the main doors of the hospital, down the driveway and out into the crowded streets, where he hailed a gharry and in less than 20 minutes was with us in the restaurant. I must say I was taken aback by his appearance: he was a most extraordinary sight. The two girls whom I had invited were in hysterics, and it was not until Rex took his wig off that the proprietor of the restaurant would allow him to join the party, and even then he thought it would be wiser to give us a table in an alcove.

Anyway, the evening was a great success, and I managed to keep Rex in order and see that he did not get up to any of his pranks, so, luckily, the other diners were not treated to any of his impersonations which might have led to his identity being discovered. He obviously enjoyed the food that I had ordered, and I could not help wondering how his newly repaired stomach was going to stand up to the strain.

None of us realised how time was getting on until the waiter came with the chit and said that they were shutting up. This brought three of us to earth with a crash. Not so Rex; he was completely unconcerned. I was worried how we were going to get him back into the hospital. The bill settled, we set off, all squeezed into a couple of gharries. These we paid off a short distance from the hospital gates, which were closed.

There was a light in the porter's lodge, but Rex did not fancy going that way, so he led us along the edge of the high wall which surrounded the place and, selecting what he thought was a suitable spot, got me to heave him up on my shoulders, and with our combined shoves he was over the top and we heard him drop onto some soft ground on the other side. There was nothing more we could do but leave him to it.

I visited the hospital a bit apprehensively the next afternoon, and he told me the sequel, very well pleased with himself and the evening's adventure. His two friends in the adjacent beds had passed an anxious time before he returned apparently without any trouble. They told him that while he was out the night nurse came round, bent over Rex's bed and addressed the dummy: "Now then Mr Warneford, how is it that you have not taken your medicine? Answer me at once. I know you are awake for I can hear you sniggering!" and she flounced out.

When eventually Rex did leave the hospital he revealed the whole story to Sister.

"Get on with you," she said, "That's a likely one!"

She had not believed a single word of it.'

SS 'Nagoya'

7

The SS Mina Brea

On June 26th 1913, after three weeks' sick leave, Rex joined the P&O-Orient Lines' *SS Nagoya* as supernumerary Fourth Officer when she docked at Calcutta on her maiden voyage from England to Australia. He had no intention of returning in her to Tilbury, and decided to leave her when she reached Melbourne. There, on 10th September, he transferred to his old friend the *SS Somali* which was about to cross the Pacific to San Francisco. During this voyage he grew tired of the life on large liners and was, in his own words, 'fed up with answering stupid questions from idle women about the workings of the ship', not to mention the approaches from grass widows, and single girls on the look out for a flirtation. He got the reputation of being an arrogant young man, and earned for the first time the nickname of 'Lone Wolf'.

When the *Somali* berthed at San Francisco on 21st December he signed off and went ashore to look around the docks for a ship, and shipmates, more suited to his taste. He soon found a small oil tanker taking on a cargo of crude oil, so Rex hailed one of her crew, went aboard, and asked to see the captain.

This ship was the *Mina Brea*. Built in 1909 for the London & Pacific Petroleum Co Ltd by the Greenock & Grangemouth Dockyard Company she was an oil tanker of 4145 tons gross and a length of 360.3 feet. The captain, a burly Scot named Walsh with a red beard and the general appearance of one who had lived his entire life at sea, greeted Rex with enthusiasm. His First Officer had only that morning been taken ashore sick and would not be able to sail on this voyage. The whole ship reeked of oil, and it was obvious that Rex's smart uniform would not be suitable for his new job as the *Mina Brea's* second officer, but he felt very much at home as he went below to the cabin he was to share with Mr R A Pigg, the navigating officer, who was affectionately known as 'Piggy'.

As Rex went down the wharf carrying his slop bag he thought the *Mina Brea* had a workmanlike look about her, no fuss and top-hamper. The crew, hanging over her rail and exchanging pleasantries with the waterfront girls, reminded him of the men who crewed the coastal vessels of the British India Steam Navigation Company. There would be no formality here, everyone would muck in and share grease rags. On Christmas day 1913 the *Mina Brea*, with a full complement of 25, sailed out through the Golden Gate in a blinding snowstorm. The crew ate their Christmas dinner of tinned goose and plummy duff, washed down with a noggin of rum, when and where they could, as the half-laden tanker clawed her way southwards into the teeth of a gale.

She was bound for Callao in Peru to pick up the rest of her cargo of oil before setting out for England. As she crept into the port with its yellow washed houses and bare dusty soil, the air was pungent with sulphur from the hot springs which bubbled out of the water, a perpetual reminder of the menace of earthquakes and tidal waves which threatened the town and harbour. Here the ship spent a week coaling for her long voyage, and taking on the last tankloads of crude oil, until she lay heavy in the water, her Plimsoll line barely visible.

She steamed sluggishly out of Callao and steered south down the coast of South America, eventually rounding Cape Horn in a blizzard. Rex had no regrets at exchanging the comfort of a crack P&O liner for the slippery decks of a tanker as she fought her way through small pack-ice and icy fog. The weather improved as they rounded the Horn and they tied up at Birkenhead without any the worse mishap than a few sprung rivets.

With three weeks leave ahead and money in his pocket, Rex boarded a train for London, and from there made his way to his aunt Maude's house in Ealing. Though grandfather Tom had now been dead for nearly eight years, Ealing was still the only home Rex knew.

Aunt Maude had aged, and his cousins were no longer at home; Meta was engaged to be married. He sat in the drawing-room trying to catch up with the events which had happened since he went away. He had left Ealing as a small, nervous schoolboy and now returned a tall, very confident young man. He asked for news of his mother. It was more than 11 years since they had last seen each other when they were parted on the station platform at Darjeeling. Since then he had only sent her occasional postcards from various parts of the world, the last one from South America. He learnt from aunt Maude that she was now living at Woolwich where Colonel Corkery was stationed, so he decided to go down and see them.

He went by train and eventually found the house where his family was staying. The door was opened by his sister Dorothy, who did not recognize him. Then he saw his mother. She came into the hall, uncertain who had called — it was a rather awkward meeting: hard to bridge the gap of so many years — and Rex found that he did not know what to say to her! He met his two young stepbrothers, and his younger sister Vi who had only been a baby when he last saw her. His two elder sisters were away in Brussels. The visit was very short, and all the things he had meant to say were never spoken; he had travelled so far away. It was sad that he felt he did not belong to them any more: they had made their lives without him. He left saying rather stiff goodbyes, and before his stepfather returned from his duties.

Rex stayed on for the rest of his leave at aunt Maude's. He was on his own once more, and so used to it, that he hardly felt the loss of not belonging. He contacted a few friends connected with the P&O, wandered around London, and went to a number of shows.

England was revelling in a glorious summer. Gay, carefree London was still unaware that it was on the brink of World War One .... He felt lonely in a way. He had never had a steady girl-friend, and he had come to believe in the proverb 'He travels fastest who travels alone'. This was to be his conviction until the day of his death.

His leave soon passed. Rex travelled back to Liverpool. The *Mina Brea*, with Rex now promoted to First Officer, sailed at the end of July for Cardiff to coal then, in ballast, pointed her bow south-west towards America, where as usual she was to fill her tanks with crude oil. Her sailing orders were to avoid the main shipping lines and to take the old trade route. When she was half-way across the Atlantic she picked up news from a passing ship that war had been declared between England and Germany. As she had no orders to the contrary she proceeded on course, passed through the Panama Canal, and then headed northwards. Captain Walsh had been warned that all British ships were to keep close inshore as the enemy were stopping all merchantmen, and confiscating their cargoes.

The *Mina Brea* arrived late in August at San Francisco, and early in September 1914 took on half the oil cargo as usual, then started for Callao to top up with the rest. With his ship now heavily laden, the captain obeyed orders to continue south towards Cape Horn, keeping within the three mile limit as much as possible in order to avoid any German war vessel which might be in the vicinity, and to call at Tocopilla for further instructions. From there orders were given to proceed to Antofagasta, 120 miles further south. A sense of emergency pervaded the ship as it travelled by night, blacked out to avoid detection, for every floating branch was the possible periscope of a U-boat, every smudge of smoke on the horizon an armed raider. Cautiously following their plotted course the officers on the bridge strained their eyes through the darkness as the ship steamed ahead at half speed. They had not been informed that the Chilean Government had shifted the light at Angamos Point, and expected that dawn would find them within sight of the bay and the sheltered harbour at Antofagasta. Suddenly, at 4.10am on the morning of September 19th, the sound of waves breaking ahead warned them of danger. Before orders could be shouted down the speaking tube to reverse engines, they had run aground.

The bows of the *Mina Brea* rose and fell back with a grinding crash. She surged forward and fell away. The engine telegraph rang 'Stop Engines', but too late. She was driven hard and fast onto the Lagatos Bank, off Tetas Point, on a falling tide. Everyone was ordered up on deck. The ship lurched and shuddered to the long rolling Pacific swell. What happened next is described by Rex in this account which he sent to his family:

'I gave orders to launch boats. The men obeyed coolly, and the falls were loosed. The boats dropped into the water alongside the ship. At this time no one got into them.

'There did not seem to be any immediate danger of the ship sinking. She was well and truly fast on the reef and the tide was falling. We hoped that, if she was not too badly damaged, we might float her off when the tide made, but if she started to break up there was nothing for us but to take to the boats. We could barely see from one end of the ship to the other, as we could not show any lights. To make matters worse we were not at all sure of our position. The wind kept light: we could hear the sound of the plates grinding on the reef as the stem of the ship rose and fell in the swell. A considerable amount of oil was leaking into the sea, and Chief reported several feet of water in the engine room. We could not tell how long she would stand being lifted bodily off the rocks by the waves, and then being slapped down again.

'We shut off the steam and put the pumps to work. It seemed, in spite of the punishment she was receiving, the water was not making too fast. After a most uncomfortable four hours, to everyone's amazement she floated clear on the rising tide. She had a fair list to starboard, and we could not tell how badly she was damaged below the water line. We pumped out a bit of oil to take the tops off the waves, which were beginning to break.

'We then started the engines, hoping that they would not fall through her. She came off the reef stern first without any trouble. Dawn was breaking and we could make out where we were. Fifteen miles to the southward across Chimba Bay lay Antofagasta. We now had to get the crippled ship across a stretch of water, where sudden storms were known to descend from the mountains and whip up the waters of the bay in a matter of minutes. We cautiously increased steam until we were limping along at about $3\frac{1}{2}$ knots, and towed the boats astern in case she foundered.

The pumps were kept at full strength, but now that the ship was moving the water was gaining, and was washing over the scuppers on the starboard side. We had practically no way on her, and she responded very sluggishly to her helm. We were a sitting duck to any enemy vessel who sighted us now.

'We struggled on towards the port whose white houses could now be clearly seen on the green hillsides. People began to congregate on the quay, to watch the unusual sight of a ship practically on her beam ends approaching the harbour. Boats put off to ask if they could render any assistance, but this we refused, as it was safer to bring her in under her own steam. Oil in a long streak marked her passage across the Bay, and as we came alongside the quay she was awash from her high stern to her forepeak. Even in the calm water of the inner harbour, there was still the possibility that she might go down under us any minute. The rest of the day and the next night the pumps were kept going. When our crew packed in, the local dockers manned them. When morning came she was still afloat, but seemed to us to be lower in the water. Divers went down to report and do some emergency repairs. It was obvious that she would have to go into dry dock. The locals who helped with the pumps could not be persuaded to stay on board at night, but not one of our crew asked to be allowed to sleep ashore.

'She became a nine day's wonder, and crowds came down daily to watch the progress of the work on her, and wagged their heads at the foolhardiness of British sailors who proposed taking her to sea again in her condition. As there was no dry dock at Antofagasta large enough to accommodate her, she would be obliged to seek another port or have to be written off as a total loss. Captain Walsh, and I am sure none of us, had any intention of this happening to her.'

For several days it was not certain that the *Mina Brea* could be saved, even with two tugs helping to pump her out, but on September 23rd an agreement was made with the firm of Orchard Gallardo for salvage to be undertaken using the compressed air technique.

A local Chilean newspaper published this report of the situation: 'The ship arrived in port with the water just about a foot below the decks and has slowly gone down before our eyes for want of some efficient method of salvaging her, until yesterday, when the officers and crew were still doing their best in the most cheerful way possible, in spite of the fact that they have had little sleep since the stranding of the ship. Thanks to the air process which has now been adopted, the vessel is slowly rising out of the water again, and there seems to be some hope for her and for those on board.

'It will, no doubt, be a surprise for our readers to know that there are past masters of the sea who have refused to stay on board a single night whilst the ship has been here, and yet the officers have offered to take the ship from here to Callao in her present condition, so as to enable her to be repaired in a dry dock. We must certainly say that every man who has had the honour to meet any of the officers of the 'Mina Brea' should always be proud of the fact, as they are the finest type of British Manhood, and, as does the Editor of this paper, never wish to meet any better.'

The salvage work continued for a month. 3,000 tons of crude oil cargo were unloaded, and various compartments of the hull were emptied and sealed until, with the aid of an extra compressor, the ship floated high in the water and was quite stable. Even so, she could not be taken to the Callao dry dock because of her present draught, and had to go south to Talcahuano instead.

On October 23rd Captain Walsh finally gave orders to cast off. As the *Mina Brea* steamed out of the harbour the strains of the town band were almost drowned by the cheers of the crowd who had gathered on the quayside to watch the departure. The ship made good passage and reached her destination safely five days later, on October 28th.

Talcahuano did not have such good dockyard facilites as Callao, and it was difficult to inch the *Mina Brea* into the small dry dock there. Once she was safely installed, however, on Monday November 2nd, the ship's company had their first clear view of the extent of the damage, and found that it was even greater than the divers' reports had indicated. They were astonished that the tanker had ever managed to steam the 900 miles south from Antofagasta. The most serious damage, under number 6 tank, was an enormous hole, reported as being approximately 24ft by 44ft. Rex made a drawing showing this and the torn plates, cracks and missing rivets for Captain Walsh to include in his report to the owners.

Rex wrote to his mother about this time to let her know that he was safe and well — the accident to the *Mina Brea* had been reported only briefly in the *Times* — and he later gave her a copy of his drawing of the ship, which she carefully preserved.

A man who met Rex in Talcahuano later wrote the following to Rex's mother: 'I am writing as one who knew Rex Warneford in October last in Chile, when he was First Officer of a tanker which had just had a very narrow escape from becoming a total wreck. As I had it from him, he was on the bridge when the ship struck a reef off the coast of Chile. Warneford showed me different photographs which he had taken while the ship was in dry dock. I would not have liked to have been aboard her round the Horn and across the Atlantic after that battering.

'I enjoyed meeting him, and had the pleasure of dining with him on several occasions. He seemed a modest sort of chap, who took everything in his stride, especially if it promised excitement. I gathered that he had travelled all round the world, and he impressed me as a real sportsman. When he managed to get a few hours off, we got a couple of horses and I took him up the mountains, which I think he enjoyed. He had a great head for heights.

DE ANTOFAGASTA.-SALVATAJE DE UN VAPOR

At the end of September the 6,000 ton North American (sic) steamship *Mina Brea* entered the port of Antofagasta practically sinking and asking for help. Two small tugs belonging to the Railway Company tried without success to prevent her from sinking with their pumps. When it was considered a lost cause the Chilean firm Orchard Gallardo succeeded in salvaging her with their powerful air compressors for £8,000.

1. Two steam tugs which attempted salvage without success.—2. The ship lying low in the water before rescue.—3. The steamer after salvage.

From the Chilean weekly 'Zig Zag'
October 31st 1914 (caption translated)

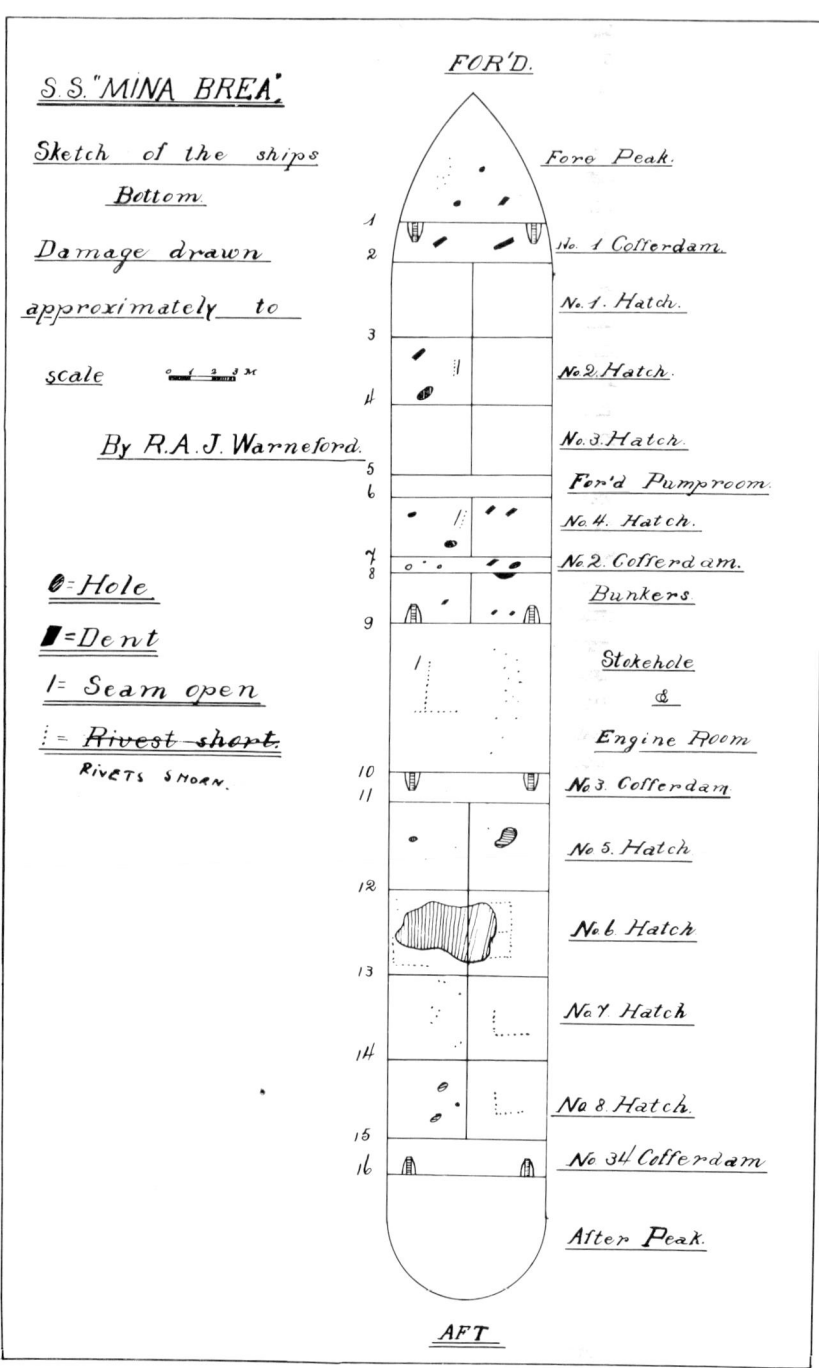

S.S. "MINA BREA"

Sketch of the ships Bottom. Damage drawn approximately to scale

By R.A.J. Warneford.

⬤ = Hole
◢ = Dent
/ = Seam open
: = ~~Rivest short~~
RIVETS SHORN.

FOR'D.

Fore Peak.
No.1 Cofferdam.
No.1 Hatch.
No.2 Hatch.
No.3 Hatch.
For'd Pumproom.
No.4 Hatch.
No.2 Cofferdam.
Bunkers
Stokehole & Engine Room
No.3 Cofferdam
No.5 Hatch
No.6 Hatch
No.7 Hatch
No.8 Hatch.
No.3&4 Cofferdam
After Peak.

AFT

48

'He left about the middle of November while the ship was being repaired. I saw him off and was really sorry to say goodbye to him. I told him we would fix up a little get-together in Berlin after a successful conclusion of the war. But I never saw him again.'

Soon after the *Mina Brea* got to Talcahuano, the battle of Coronel took place on the evening of November 1st between Admiral von Spee's Pacific squadron and a smaller British force under the command of Admiral Sir Christopher Cradock. Two British cruisers, the *Good Hope* and the *Monmouth*, were lost, with Admiral Cradock and about 1,600 men.

It was now clear that even temporary repairs to the *Mina Brea* would take some time, so Captain Walsh decided that the best way to inform the London and Pacific Petroleum Co of what was involved would be to send Rex straight back to England by the first available ship, with a full, accurate, firsthand account, and his drawing and photographs of the damage. Rex therefore arrived at Liverpool about the middle of December, and was able to spend Christmas 1914 with the Nightingales at Ealing.

Work on the *Mina Brea* at Talcahuano went on well, perhaps better than the owners might have expected when they received the report, for on Monday December 2nd she sailed for Callao, and finally returned to England on January 23rd, when she docked at Falmouth.

Rex never sailed again on the 'brave old lady' he had left at Talcahuano, but she was destined to survive him by 14 years, changing hands twice, and making her last voyage under the flag of a Canadian company, Imperial Oil Ltd. While sailing from Halifax to Dalhousie in August 1929, she caught fire and was abandoned. Later the fire was extinguished, and on August 16th she was towed into Halifax, Nova Scotia. She was sold to the breakers and finally broken up at Sydney, Cape Breton, a charred and burnt-out shell.

Drawing of the 'Mina Brea' given by Rex to his mother (original 17 x 10 ins)

Recruiting advertisement, 1915.

8

A Period of Training

Rex was able to leave the merchant service, which had not been made a reserved occupation at that time, and seek some other way of serving his country. He would naturally have preferred to remain at sea, for the sea had been his life for so long, and he knew his own abilities; but when he tried to join the submarine service he was rejected, because he did not have the correct Royal Navy background or training at Dartmouth College. Greatly disappointed, he had to fall back on the army. Perhaps one of the recruiting posters or press advertisements of the time caught his eye as he journeyed to London: however it came about, he decided to volunteer for one of the Sportsman's Battalions which seemed to offer something a little different from foot-slogging in an infantry regiment. There might be a 'bit of excitement' in it, even as second best to the submarine service.

The Sportsman's Battalions were attached to the Royal Fusiliers, and had been conceived at the outbreak of the war by Mrs E Cunliffe-Owen who had approached the War Office and gained permission to form a group of men aged between 19 and 45 who were required to be 'by reason of their lives as sportsmen, fit and hard'. Recruiting was carried out in a wooden building outside the Hotel Cecil in the Strand, London.

On January 8th 1915 Rex went along for an interview. He entered the hut whose walls were pasted with lurid propaganda posters and slogans, and approached the desk. The recruiting sergeant, a blustering, heavily-moustached fellow obviously impressed with his job, bellowed 'Why do you want to join?'

Rex stared up at a poster behind the sergeant's head: it showed a young girl handing a white feather to a seedy-looking individual in civilian clothes, with the caption ARE YOU DOING YOUR BIT?

'To do MY bit', replied Rex, tongue in cheek, suiting his words to the poster with a poker-faced expression. There was a pause; the sergeant was not quite sure of his ground with this young man, and started his next question a little less belligerently:

'Are you willing to serve abroad for three or four years, or for the duration of the war?'

Rex nodded his head, and to the next queries as to whether he could walk fast, ride a horse or a bicycle, swim and shoot (no particular weapon specified) he answered in the affirmative. Still very uncertain in his mind whether this would offer him the sort of excitement he craved, though at least he appeared to be qualified, Rex signed his name on the form and was enlisted in the 2nd Sportsman's

Battalion. Then he was sent on to the clothing store where he was issued with a khaki uniform which did not fit, yards of puttees, and heavy dubbined army boots. The man who kitted him out patted him on the shoulder in paternal fashion and said 'Now laddie, you're a real soldier'. Rex's reply has not been recorded.

Alas for adventure and 'excitement'. Rex was in for a sad awakening. The new recruits were sent en bloc via Victoria station to a gloomy mansion near Horsham called Grey Towers, where life fell far short of any sort of excitement. It was dismal in the extreme, 'a sort of Boy Scouts' Jamboree for old gentlemen' was how Rex described it.

Many of the sportsmen, culled as required from all members of society, looked well over the stipulated age, but were still brisk of step and bright of eye for the time being. Yet when their training included route marches over the sodden and freezing Sussex countryside they visibly wilted and caught cold, and the Sportsman's Battalions were well below strength till the next draft rolled up, the older ones again dropping out with steady regularity. Rex and the younger and hardier individuals survived to be sent to another God-forsaken place near Clipstone.

These men were handpicked (by a superannuated sergeant who had done yeoman service in the Boer War) for the honour of being styled a 'crack unit': 'it was cracked all right, very nearly shattered', opined Rex who was at his wits' end having to spend his evenings listening to pep talks from ancient colonels on hand to hand combat. It seemed unlikely that any of them had experienced what they so blood-thirstily described. Nor did he think that any of their advice would be of much assistance to those soon to embark for the 'real thing' in northern France and the Low Countries. The 'cracked unit' was told that it would shortly be on the move again, this time for a transit camp.

Rex was now determined that he must get out of this 'suicide squad' before they could send him to some remote training establishment, said to be in the Scottish highlands, from where he did not think there would be any hope of his emerging except as a raving lunatic. He therefore came to a decision to try to join the Royal Naval Air Service, which he had not even considered before, because he now felt that there he really could serve his country, find excitement, and be near the sea again: so he confronted his Commanding Officer with a request for transfer. It was, to his surprise and gratification, granted with alacrity; in fact the CO expedited Rex's departure by adding a memo to the RNAS saying he expected that Warneford's career with them was likely to be, to say the least, 'illuminating'.

The Royal Naval Air Service had officially come into being on June 26th 1914. Previously the Naval Wing of the Royal Flying Corps, it ceased to be associated with the Military Wing (administered by the War Office) and thereafter comprised all naval aircraft and personnel, administered by the Admiralty. Whereas the role of the Royal Flying Corps was to support the Army in defence of the front lines, the main concern of the RNAS in co-operation with the Navy was the defence of Britain and the area around the coast from sea and air attack.

A clear idea of what would be required of such a service had already formed in the mind of Mr Winston Churchill, then First Lord of the Admiralty, when on March 17th 1914 he said 'Passive defence against such attack is perfectly hopeless and endless. You would have to roof in the world to be quite sure ... The only real security upon which sound military principles will rely is that you should be master of your own air'. His preoccupation with the problems of air defence was of long standing, and already in October 1913 he had given consideration to possible methods of action against a Zeppelin 'which should be attacked by an aeroplane descending on it obliquely from above, and discharging a series of small bombs or fireballs, at rapid intervals, so that a string of them, more than a hundred yards in length, would be drawn like a whiplash across the gas bag'.

The service built up against this background of concern had its first opportunity to demonstrate its use in connection with naval operations during the Review of the Fleet at Spithead by the King in July 1914. All available land-based aircraft were flown in formation over the assembled fleet, which for the first time included seventeen seaplanes actually moored in lines with the naval vessels.

By January 1915 the RNAS was severely stretched in its defensive role: surface raiders had shelled Scarborough and Hartlepool in December; the battleship *Formidable* had been sunk off the Isle of Wight by a submarine; and the first Zeppelins had raided the coast at Yarmouth. Such was the state of affairs when Rex applied to join the service on February 10th 1915.

The RNAS accepted him at face value, as a probationary pilot without demur. He was to find the 'bit of excitement' that he was looking for, but his new path was not going to be an easy one. He had never flown before, and he had no theoretical knowledge of aeronautics. Probationary pilots had to pass a stiff medical examination before acceptance, but were also assessed for above average intelligence, iron nerves, and initiative. Rex qualified on all counts, and was sent to the civilian school at Hendon where pupils were instructed in basic flying to obtain their Royal Aero Club Aviator's Certificate before being transferred to the Central Flying School, Upavon or to Eastchurch, for further training.

To gain his certificate a prospective pilot was first given ground instruction in the handling of all controls, after which he learnt to taxi the machine on the airfield. Having gained this experience he was then taken up with an instructor and the science of flight demonstrated in practice. Next, in a machine equipped with dual controls, he had the opportunity to take over, feel how the aircraft handled, and practise take-offs and landings. When the instructor felt his pupil was sufficiently experienced he was allowed to go solo — the supreme test. Conduct and progress were regularly reported and if, after a few weeks, the pupil failed to come up to requirements he would be swiftly transferred to some other branch of the service. If the pupil succeeded in passing all tests and examinations without mishap he would obtain his flying certificate and could put up his wings.

Rex managed to make the grade in less than five weeks and was granted his Royal Aero Club Certificate No 1098 on February 25th 1915, but his probationary period had not been without its difficulties. He was not a good mixer and was not easily accepted by his fellow probationers, who had backgrounds very different from his own. He suffered from an inferiority complex, not because he felt he lacked ability, but because his own lack of conventional education cut him off from the boys who had joined up fresh from their public schools and colleges. He was miles away from their secure and traditional world.

On days when he was not needed at the base he whistled up the camp's red setter

and trudged off to explore the countryside. If his fellow fliers had only taken the trouble to find out what he was really like, he would have been glad to make friends as he had with the crews of his ships. Less than 12 months later some of them, recalling his isolation, may have felt a twinge of remorse.

His instructor at Hendon was Flight Lieutenant Warren Merriam. Merriam was one of the pre-war pioneer airmen and a great war-time flying instructor. Strangely, he was extremely short-sighted, and once mistook a very senior Admiralty official, carrying two briefcases across the airfield, for a mechanic with a couple of petrol cans. The ensuing argument grew quite heated until his error was pointed out. Merriam thought very highly of Rex as a pilot and felt he was a born aviator, having rapidly mastered the art of flying, and being quite fearless. His principal fault was over-confidence, which did nothing to endear him to his fellow pupils, or to Squadron Commander Sitwell. Sitwell was a disciplinarian of the traditional naval school, extremely strict in his outlook, who was convinced that Rex would never make officer material and intended to send in a report to this effect. Rex had indeed disgraced himself on one occasion by landing one precious training machine on top of another, thereby writing them both off. Merriam, not wishing to lose a most promising pupil, wondered what he could do to help, and was fortunately able to bring Rex's flying qualities to the attention of a more sympathetic senior officer, Commander R M Groves.

Commander Groves, or 'Crasher' Groves, as he was affectionately known, had earned his nickname when appointed Officer Commanding Naval Air Stations by insisting on undertaking flying training, during the course of which he managed to smash more aircraft than any other pupil. He was respected and popular at his job which included visiting training establishments to check potential pilots, for which he had a keen eye. He was seldom wrong in his judgement.

During a chance visit to Hendon Merriam seized the opportunity and instructed Rex to show Groves what he could do: 'I got him a Bristol biplane, and warned him to give the show of his young life. He responded magnificently, so much so that Groves and his staff were most impressed by the young pilot's handling of his machine, causing the Commander to remark: "This youngster will either do big things or kill himself." It was tragic that when the time came he was unable to achieve the first without falling a victim to the second.'

Opposite: Rex as a newly-qualified Flight Sub-Lieutenant at Hendon in front of a Maurice Farman 11.

Henry Farman F22 at Upavon, March 1914.

Squadron Commander Sitwell in a Voisin LA at Hendon

9

Warneford Place

With a mixture of relief and apprehension, Hendon passed Rex on to the Central Flying School at Upavon, Wiltshire. He was warned, as his CO handed him his papers, that he would be wise to curb his impetuosity in the future.

During the period he was stationed there, Rex decided to make a pilgrimage to the hamlet of Sevenhampton where the Warnefords had first set down their roots. He had bought himself a two-seater sports car, painted bright red. He was very proud of it, and had stripped it down to the bare shell and rebuilt it. There was no hood, windscreen or side-screens, and with his foot hard down on the accelerator 'fifty miles an hour could be got out of her, and more downhill!'

The manor, Warneford Place, was situated a few miles north-east of Swindon. It had been sold in 1902 by Rex's cousin John Warneford and was now in the possession of Sir Frederick Banbury, one of the directors of the Great Western Railway, which had its engineering sheds and carriage works in nearby Swindon. He had bought the place so that he could be near the works, and because it also offered ideal surroundings for breeding and training horses. His son was a keen horseman, and his daughter Evelyn was one of the very few women who could handle a four-in-hand, and drove his fine team of chestnuts to a park drag. She rode side-saddle, and was as courageous as her brother Charles.

Young Captain Charles Banbury rode for his regiment. He had a successful string of steeplechasers including a dark bay gelding, Noble Roy, on which he won, among other races, the Grand Military Cup at Aldershot on April 26th, 1911. But Warneford Place did not fulfil the purpose for which it was bought. Charles was killed in action in France during the second month of the war. His parents and sister never recovered from his death, and the suite of rooms that he occupied was kept exactly as the day he left for the front.

Evelyn never hunted again, though Noble Roy and the second charger which had accompanied Charles to France were sent back to Warneford and turned out in the park. Noble Roy lived on till the commencement of the second World War without ever again having a saddle on his back. These details, and the description of Rex's visit to Warneford Place, were related to the author by Miss Banbury.

One morning when he was free of duties Rex set off. The roads were crowded with army transport, columns of marching men, long strings of horses, gun limbers and all types of service wagons. Fast, camouflaged open staff cars passed in clouds of dust bearing red-tabbed officers to 'urgent' destinations. In Marlborough he stopped to ask the way, and after three-quarters of an hour on the road to Highworth, he turned right at a signpost marked Sevenhampton.

As he drove slowly down an avenue lined by tall leafless elms he would have seen, through white painted gates, acre after acre of pasture, rich brown fallows, and short-cropped winter leys, sheltered on their eastern boundaries by wooded copses. As his eyes took in the scene he must have recognized the landmarks so often described by grandfather Tom. He was not surprised that his forbears had fought to keep these lands through strife, sudden death and crippling poverty; the situation of the estate was its greatest beauty.

To the south, the high ridge of the Downs sheltered the strange form of the White Horse of Uffington, cut in the green turf long ago when England was young. Below the dark shadowed vale, which takes its name from the equine creature above, the contour of the hills to the east descended into the wooded valley where the chimneys of the manor could be seen through the lacework of bare branches. North of the house lay the village of Sevenhampton, so named from the seven homesteads, dating from the time of William the Conqueror, which were mentioned in the Domesday Book.

Since the outbreak of war the village often seemed deserted. Those inhabitants not called to the forces were working in the fields or the long timber sheds. The centuries-old trees were being felled all over the estate and hauled there by teams of heavy horses, to be sawn up to build camps and fortifications throughout the country.

Rex arrived at the front door of Warneford Place just before 12 o'clock. He was greeted by a pack of small Shetland sheepdogs which belonged to Lady Banbury. The old butler showed him into the morning room where Evelyn Banbury, dressed in mourning, was sitting at a desk strewn with papers. She explained that she was acting secretary for her father who, since her brother had been killed, had become more and more dependent on her. It was not possible to show Rex the house, but she took him to the foot of the staircase where a tall window, filled with stained glass coats of arms, reached to the second storey. One pane which was to bear the Banbury coat was missing, but the others had been taken from various windows all over the house and bore the escutcheons of long dead Warnefords. Rex did not have much time to study them, for Miss Banbury took him outside to show him the gardens and the lake behind the house.

They walked across the wide lawns followed by the pack of little dogs, the silver waters of the lake on their left mirroring the overhanging trees and shrubs. The fountain in the centre of the lawn, guarded by five stone herons, had ceased to play and the formal flower beds were bare, but under the sheltered banks which enclosed the gardens snowdrops hung their delicate heads, while celandines and wild violets formed a tapestry interwoven with dark green ivy leaves. Rex heard the story of the ghost of Sir Charles Wetherell who was said to haunt the walk beside the lake. In a mossy hollow under an ancient yew tree she showed him a cluster of little tombstones, the graves of many dogs which had belonged to generations of the families living at the manor. Evelyn drew aside a low branch which sheltered the most imposing memorial of them all inscribed 'Here lies Zoë, favourite Blenheim Spaniel of Lady Warneford'.

Warneford Place, Sevenhampton, Wilts. A view of the house as Rex saw it in 1915 with the alterations made to the central block for the Banbury family. This house was built between 1768 and 1772 for Catherine, wife of the Rev Francis Warneford, to replace a Tudor mansion which had fallen into disrepair. The 18th-century building was demolished in 1960 and a modern house now stands on the site.

As they said goodbye in front of the old house she told Rex how much she had enjoyed meeting him, saying that he would be very welcome if he came again. She then directed him to the parish church in Highworth. Rex had some lunch before crossing the square to the Church of St Michael, where the Warneford chapel stood in the south aisle. The verger who took him round later remembered the young airman's visit. He had shown him the Warneford memorials, some with Latin epitaphs, and some in mediaeval English like the one of Elizabeth Warneford which read 'Who died in the beautie of her daies and the sparklings of glory'.

It was late in the afternoon when he drove back to Upavon, and his mind must have been filled with the sights and memories of the day. But soon, engaged in the activities of his urgent training programme, the serenity of the enchanted place took on the semblance of a dream. Four months later Evelyn Banbury read, with a sense of almost personal loss, of the valiant deed and the death of the boy who had spent a short hour with her in the gardens of her home. She had often thought of him but he, caught up in his rapid and dangerous life, may have forgotten her.

Soon after his visit to Warneford Place Rex completed his training at Upavon and was posted to No 2 Squadron RNAS at Eastchurch. The Eastchurch Station was on a rather desolate aerodrome on the Isle of Sheppey, separated from the mainland of Kent by the Swale, and from the south coast of Essex by the much wider Thames estuary. In addition to being an advanced training establishment Eastchurch also defended this area against aerial attack, and was carrying out experimental wireless co-operation with naval vessels in gunnery spotting off the coast.

Because of his nature, which had stopped him from mixing easily with his fellow officers at Hendon and Upavon, Rex had gradually earned the reputation of being an over-confident and positively cocky individual, rather wild and uncivilized. This had preceded him to Eastchurch where he was given a rather chilly reception, but being used to it by now he was no longer upset by it. On the contary, it would seem to have fostered the devil in him for he decided to live up to what he took to be expected of him on arrival.

As he paused in the doorway of the long wooden hut which served as the Officers' Mess, all eyes were turned towards him. Rex strode into the middle of the room, pulled out his revolver, twirled it round in his hand cowboy fashion and said, in the deep south American drawl which he liked to affect 'Hi suckers! What about this?' Then he fired six shots up into the roof. Nobody moved or spoke. Rex replaced his gun in its holster, turned on his heel and left the Mess. As soon as the door closed behind him all hell broke loose. They were shocked, very angry, and at a loss. They decided to have nothing to do with him for the rest of his stay at Eastchurch. They had certainly heard about him, but they were not prepared for him to be worse than he had been painted. Ben Travers, famous after the war for his productions of the Aldwych farces, was stationed there at that time. He was a big-hearted courageous type, and very sociable. He never could make anything of Rex who he thought was American, and was annoyed by his brash and cocksure nature.

Squadron Commander E L Gerrard, in charge of the Station, also found Rex's behaviour a problem, but his lack of orthodox discipline was counterbalanced by his excellent flying abilities, and he never damaged an aircraft although he appeared to fly recklessly — and always alone.

One man who did appreciate Rex's peculiar qualities, and saw through the wild introverted character that he affected to preserve the isolation which was now necessary to him, was an instructor, Flight Lieutenant Mike Marsden, who described Rex in these words: 'It would be difficult to find a wilder or more untameable individual than Rex Warneford. He is like a thoroughbred colt. I first met him in the early days at Hendon, when he was in the making. Even then, his efficiency and bravery were never in question. If it had not been for this, he would never have survived the place, with its strict discipline in the Navy tradition. But he did.'

Gerrard also recognized that Rex had the makings of a first class fighting airman and that if he remained at Eastchurch he would be lucky to get into action before someone wrung his neck, so it was arranged to send him out to France as soon as possible. On the morning of May 7th 1915 therefore, Rex climbed into an Avro 504, drew down his goggles, and set off to join No 1 Squadron RNAS, based at Dunkirk. His short stay in England was at an end.

Opposite: Comander Samson's Eastchurch Squadron at Dunkirk in 1914

10

The Aerodrome at St Pol

One of the first roles performed by the RNAS on the outbreak of war was escorting the British Expeditionary Forces to the continent. A regular seaplane patrol was therefore maintained between Westgate, Kent and Ostend in Belgium, where a temporary base was established on August 13th 1914. Due to the swift advance of the German forces towards Belgium this seaplane base was forced to withdraw on August 22nd, when occupation of Ostend seemed imminent. However, every opportunity for offensive action being sought, on the 27th the 'Eastchurch Squadron' under Commander C R Samson was sent to Ostend in support of a Brigade of Royal Marines who were landed to occupy the town. Samson's squadron consisted of ten various aircraft plus a miscellaneous collection of lorries and hastily improvised armoured touring cars.

After three days both the Marine Brigade and the squadron were ordered back to England, but Samson sent his aircraft only as far back as Dunkirk. Here, by means of liaison with the French, he established a depot at St Pol which adjoined the town, and eventually succeeded in receiving instructions from the Admiralty to operate from there, to carry out aerial patrols against Zeppelins and aeroplanes, and reconnaissance as required by the French General at Dunkirk. Thus, on September 1st, two days before officially taking over the air defence of Great Britain, the Admiralty had established an air base at Dunkirk from which the offensive operations of attacking airship sheds, submarine bases, and artillery reconnaissance could be carried out.

On October 11th the Dover Patrol took over control of the Straits while some of their monitors, firing from the sea, attempted to stem the forward rush of Germans along the coast, but by the end of October the enemy had occupied Belgium and were establishing submarine bases and airship sheds in preparation for their attack on England. Dunkirk became the centre for the whole naval air effort against the enemy.

By early 1915 the submarine menace was becoming serious. A German Admiralty bulletin issued on February 4th stated that from the 18th onwards all waters around the British Isles would be regarded as a war zone. This announcement of a submarine blockade led to the immediate concentration of naval aircraft for the bombing of Belgian bases. Aircraft and seaplanes from various Stations were sent to reinforce No 1 Squadron RNAS at Dover, and those at Dunkirk, for a series of raids planned from February 11th, but due to the limited aircraft at the Admiralty's disposal the bombing of the bases was little more than a demonstration.

No 1 Squadron* RNAS had been formed at Fort Grange, Gosport on October 14th 1914, and by the end of January 1915 had transferred to Dover where training was completed. Under Wing Commander Arthur M Longmore the Squadron was officially transferred to Dunkirk on February 26th, to replace Samson's unit which was withdrawn to Dover prior to embarking for the eastern Mediterranean campaign in the Dardanelles.

General view of St Pol aerodrome with anti-aircraft defences in the foreground

Their duties at Dunkirk were (1) To endeavour to prevent Zeppelins and aircraft operating from bases in Belgium for raids on England. (2) To attack enemy submarines using Ostend and Zeebrugge and to obtain information as to their movements. (3) To co-operate with the Dover Patrol and their monitors, both in spotting for them and in protecting them from aerial attack. (4) To obtain information on enemy shipping movements by coastal reconnaissance. (5) To develop aerial photography and wireless communication from aircraft under active

*In June 1915 Nos 1, 2 and 3 Squadrons were designated Wings, the word squadron being reserved for a group of six aircraft.

Fitter Albert Hawkins examining a Nieuport after a heavy landing

service conditions. 'These duties we carried out to the best of our ability' wrote Wing Commander Longmore, 'with the primitive equipment at our disposal, and with the small number of officer pilots and aeroplanes available. As far as possible, pilots were allotted to specific tasks and their initiative and enterprise were beyond all praise.*

Conditions at this time were recalled by Albert E Hawkins who, with his younger brother, was a fitter at the base. 'A few of us were lucky enough to get a bed in the old buildings, but many had to do with palliasses in tents throughout the icy months of February and March, when at last things began to improve. The officers, for whom there was insufficient accommodation on the field, messed and slept on the old cross-channel steamer *Empress,* moored alongside the jetty at Dunkirk near the seaplane base.'

The great significance of the work of the Dover Patrol may be judged from the fact that over 5,600,000 troops were transported to France without accident or loss of a single man. Admiral Sir Reginald Bacon, Commander of the Dover Patrol, described the duties they undertook: 'When, during 1915, the German mine-laying submarines became active, the whole of the traffic routes had to be swept by trawlers. They usually began to sweep their sections at first sign of daylight and

*From Sea to Sky p46, Geoffrey Bles, 1946

63

continued until each section had been cleared both ways. The sweep covered a width of half a mile. The first paddle minesweepers arrived at Dover in 1915, under Commander Rigg RN ... They were the safest vessels for sweeping owing to their shallow draft and their speed of 10 to 11 knots, which enabled them to sever the moorings of the German mines cleanly and safely. These then floated to the surface and did not remain entangled in the sweep. The only difficulty was their inability to sweep efficiently in rough weather. Trawlers drawing up to 15 feet of water suffered many losses on patrol, while the paddle steamers, drawing a maximum of 8 or 9 feet, were at least 25% safer than the trawlers.'

Rex's first cousin John Robert Kemys Warneford* was in command of the paddle minesweeper *Albion.* He was a few years older than Rex, over six feet tall and possessed 'bags of charm and was as wild as they come'. When the *Albion* was in Dunkirk harbour JRKW met his cousin Rex on several occasions. All the ships which commuted between Dover and Dunkirk were under the constant surveillance and protection of the aeroplanes of the RNAS, and the two boys found much to talk about.

No 1 Squadron's shortage of aeroplanes and pilots was soon made up, and by the time Rex arrived it was practically at full strength, but it was not a very imposing set-up which met his eyes when he flew in to St Pol on that bright day early in May. Several planes were parked, backed on to a long building which could hardly be called a hangar, used when necessary to repair damage and to service the aircraft two at a time. Other roughly camouflaged low buildings included a briefing room and the CO's office which was nothing more than a hut.

*Father of the author

Line-up of five Nieuport 12 two-seaters and a solitary Morane Saulnier parasol. The Nieuports are unserialed, but the Union Jack on the rudder of the nearest aircraft is an interesting variation in early national markings

A typical St Pol landing accident. The victim is a Voisin

The ground was sandy and covered with tufts of grass, and earthworks surrounded the field. These frequently caused accidents to aircraft which flew too low, hit them and turned turtle. This was an almost daily occurrence with fresh pilots until they learned the lie of the land and came in more steeply. The banks were the homes of myriads of rats which afforded the pilots many happy hours when off duty, driving them out with rags dipped in paraffin and setting the dogs on them. Daily tallies were kept of how many were killed, but the rats never seemed to decrease in number and continued scavenging the camp's kitchens and stores at night.

Rex touched down with fortunately a perfect landing and made his way to the CO's office. He was not sure what his reception here would be like, but was immediately reassured by Wing Commander Longmore: 'I told him that he seemed to have an unsavoury reputation but that he would be judged solely on what he did in my squadron and not on his past record at Eastchurch. That night he drove one of my precious Talbot tenders into a ditch and damaged it severely when returning to camp: I said I would give him one more chance and if he offended again out of the squadron he would go.'

The next morning Rex was detailed for his first coastal reconnaissance flight to Zeebrugge, accompanied by an experienced observer in a slow Voisin. They headed up the coast at about 4,000 feet and shrapnel began to burst around them as they reached Ostend. The observer shouted instructions to steer a zig-zag course and head out to sea, climbing to get clear of the flak, but Rex took no notice and kept on going through the barrage towards Zeebrugge. When a German aircraft appeared, Rex immediately gave chase and it turned back towards its aerodrome at Ostend. He pursued it low over the town, firing at it with his rifle.

Meanwhile at St Pol hope of the Voisin's return was failing and after two and a half hours it was assumed they must have force landed due to lack of petrol, but

Rex's second Morane-Saulnier L, 3253, at St Pol. At the hangar entrance are two Voisin LA pusher biplanes, the type Rex flew with G E Meddis as observer

they finally returned with only a few pints of fuel left in the tank. The observer, John H D'Albiac, on reporting to Longmore 'asked me never to send him up again with this madman ... I came to the conclusion that Warneford had no fear of anything and my task from then on was to try to keep him alive as long as possible to do as much damage to the Germans as he could.'

'When I sent him and some others to locate and bomb a long-range gun which had been shelling Dunkirk for some time he came back with his plane looking like a pepperpot and very shortly reports came in from the French Front Line that some mad pilot had been cruising up and down the German lines at a few feet attacking this gun.'*

Another observer, who actually volunteered to fly with Rex, was Leading Mechanic G E Meddis. Later he described himself as unfortunate enough to be briefed to fly with Warneford, and lucky enough to survive the ordeal. During their observation flight Rex spotted a German Taube. Anything that flew was a challenge to him, so he gave chase 'like a St Bernard after a rat' in the staid Voisin and nearly drove it into the ground. Meddis recalled: 'I hung on for dear life, inwardly blaming myself for having depreciated Warneford's previous exploits, when I found myself in the hot seat sending up urgent prayers for my preservation. When my gun jammed halfway through the chase Warneford leaned out of his cockpit, letting the machine fly itself. He grabbed my gun, wrestled with it for a few minutes, got it going and handed it to me as he climbed back. He pulled us out of a dive, yelling to me to get the Taube, which be a miracle I did, and got home without a scratch.

'I will say he was a magnificent chap at the controls, and I found myself enjoying the experience in retrospect. I flew with him on several occasions after this, risking my unhappy life each time. The rest of the squadron foretold an early death for us

*Letter from ACM Sir Arthur Longmore to the author, 1956

both, but strangely enough, after the first experience, I found that I had complete confidence in him.

'On another day we were together in the Voisin again and were returning from an uneventful operation, "spotting", which had not nearly enough action for him. He flew the machine towards the old church which we were using for the gound staff and crews. How he missed it I shall never know. He headed straight into it, then yanked the Voisin, complaining in every joint, into a steep left-handed bank. The chaps inside, hearing the roar of our engine, rushed out. They told me afterwards that we were not 20 feet above them. As our undercarriage slithered past the side of the church, Rex leaned out of the cockpit and waved. They just yelled and shook their fists at us.'

'Meddis was a very brave man,' wrote Wing Commander Longmore, 'and until Rex flew single-seater aeroplanes Meddis remained with him as his observer.' The last time they flew together was on May 17th 1915.

Rex had long wanted to fly one of the fast single-seater aeroplanes, and Longmore soon decided that the time had come to give the young pilot his chance and make the most of his fighting qualities. He therefore allotted him a Morane Saulnier monoplane and gave him a roving commission to harry German observation aircraft whenever they appeared. The temperamental Morane and the special duties both suited Rex to perfection.

The Morane was an elegant if somewhat unconventional design, having a high wing with a sharp angle of incidence. It was basically a two-seater, but was flown as a single-seater from the rear cockpit, and a primitive bomb rack, specially developed by Hawkins and another fitter for single-seater use, had been bolted to the undercarriage.

Because of the unusual contruction, this machine was known as the 'Parasol' and there was something about her as frivolous as the name. She was a very 'feminine' aircraft, quick and light on the controls. The wood-framed fuselage was rectangular in section, 22′ 6″ long, and the wingspan was 36′ 9″, giving a wing area of 197 square feet. The engine was an 80 hp Gnome which accounted for more than a third of the total weight of the machine.

The single high wing above the cockpit made the design very suitable for artillery spotting and aerial photography, despite its basic instability, but a cool and courageous flier could turn it into a deadly fighting machine. The aircraft provided for Rex was one of the first to be fitted with a machine gun firing forward through the arc of the two-bladed propeller which was protected by metal deflector plates since mechanical synchronisation was not then available. About one bullet in ten would strike the propeller and be flung off by the plates. The Morane was also able to carry six 20 lb Hales bombs which would explode on impact. They were released by the pilot using a toggle and wire, which was some improvement on throwing them out by hand.

With a maximum speed of 72 mph and sometimes more at high altitudes, the Morane had a certain advantage over a Zeppelin in the air, but like all heavier than air machines of the time she was slow in climbing. It took her 27 minutes to reach 10,000 feet and at 1,000 feet her rate of climb was only 120 feet per minute, which was negligible compared with a Zeppelin's great bound of 1,000 feet per minute.

No.1 Wing group at St Pol. From left to right, back row: Sub Lt Ogston, Flt Lt Haskinson, Lt Cameron, Sub Lt Graham, Lt Nutting, Surgeon Anderson, Sub Lt Jones, Sub Lt Rose, Lt Villiers, Sub Lt Peal; middle row: Lt Evill, Sqn Cdr Bigsworth, Wing Cdr Longmore, Lt Cdr Chilcott, Lt Dyott; front row: Sub Lt Mills, Sub Lt Warneford, Lt Wilson.

Wing Commander Longmore provided the Morane because he had found the key to Rex's character. He had watched with growing confidence the young flier's progress at St Pol and like Rex's former instructors, Lieutenant Merriam and Flight Lieutenant Marsden, he had come to appreciate his peculiar talents: but his virtues and his faults were interdependent, and tragically only death would remove their contradictions.

With his new darling the Morane Rex spent many hours over the front lines attacking enemy observation aircraft and balloons. He could climb up high and then, diving at the giant sausages swaying on their mooring cables, drop his bombs onto their bulging backs and hope to see them explode into a roaring mass before floating down to earth in fiery fragments. He usually returned with some bullet holes in his aircraft which in fact was so frequently damaged that Longmore had to get a second Morane for him to use while the other was out of action. His lone attacks were naturally conspicuous, and he became known as the 'Wild Hawk'. Now Keats' words, that his father had written out for him on the fly-leaf of the old book of poems, really applied to him: like the charioteer of the poet's vision he too could revel in flight 'along a huge cloud's ridge' and wheel downward 'into fresher skies, tipt round with silver from the sun's bright eyes'. Now like the bird whose name he had been given he knew in flight the joy of being alive.

But his father's chosen quotation had also included the fading of the aerial vision and the invading 'sense of real things'; and 'real things' there were, mostly unpleasant, to confront Rex and the other members of Longmore's 'nest of young eagles'. Their average life-expectancy would be no more than three weeks as they flew out day after day over enemy territory to bomb submarine bases, railway yards, troop concentrations and Zeppelin sheds, and there was a perpetual sense of urgency at St Pol where planes were taking off at all hours of the day and night in a ceaseless round of observation and attack.

During patrols on cold moonless nights pilots experienced strange hallucinations and terrible feelings of isolation in the baffling obscurity. On such lonely vigils they often took comfort in carrying some form of mascot or talisman as their sole contact with reality. Rex, the 'Wild Hawk', had a model of a stooping falcon on the instrument panel of his Morane. Instruments were not always reliable or well illuminated, and sometimes a flier could estimate his position relative to the coast only when he was able to see the thin gleaming line of surf where waves broke along the shore.

The aircraft themselves at this time were a further hazard, as tough, eccentric and hard to handle as the men who flew them and gave them every sort of nickname from 'birdcages' to 'flaming coffins'. There were frequent crashes on the field and Fitter Hawkins took and kept many pictures of planes standing on their noses, upside down, or reduced to a tangled mass of fabric, wires and wood. The pilots who survived such experiences acquired the wiles of the fox and became more dangerous to their enemies the longer they lived to pass on their hard-earned knowledge to younger men.

In the midst of all their difficulties, Wing Commander Longmore and his men formulated their own technique to combat the enemy in the air during discussions in the briefing room: 'The rules of the game are inflexible. If you can hear a machine gun other than your own, do not wait to see what it is firing at: it is undoubtedly you. Stalk your quarry; fly high out of sight into the clouds or the sun. Keep in his blind spot, behind him and beneath his tail. Get as close to him as possible before you fire. Then fire only in short bursts.'

Now, with increasing experience to reinforce and direct his natural ability, Rex was equipped to join an heroic company of men, popularly known as the air aces, the fliers whose fame would endure.

11

The Zeppelin Menace

Lecturing to a large audience of naval personnel at Kiel in 1912 Kapitän von Pustau said: 'Let us imagine a war with England, which from time immemorial has had an unwarlike population. If we could succeed in throwing some bombs on their docks, they would speak with us in quite different terms. With airships we have the means of carrying the war into the British country.'

In July 1900 Count Ferdinand von Zeppelin's first giant airship had taken falteringly to the air from its floating hangar on Lake Constance at Friedrichshafen. Within a decade versions of his perfected brain-child were carrying thousands of paying passengers on scheduled services throughout Germany.

LZ11, 'Viktoria Luise', one of seven civil Zeppelins operated by DELAG before WWI, made 489 flights carrying a total of 2,995 paying passengers. During the war it was used for training.

The German Army and Navy were not slow to adopt this example of German genius. Initially intended for reconnaissance, both armed services soon realized the more warlike potential of the Zeppelin, as the airships had become popularly known. At the outbreak of war Germany had available seven military and three commercial Zeppelins.

Disturbing rumours of 'Germany's aerial dreadnoughts' had reached London as early as 1910 but, a year later, the War Office was 'not convinced that either aeroplanes or airships will be of any utility in war'. Yet a few months prior to the outbreak of war Winston Churchill, the new First Lord of the Admiralty, said on March 17th 'any hostile aircraft or airships which reached our coast during the coming year would be promptly attacked in superior force by a swarm of very formidable hornets' In fact neither side was capable of either mounting or repelling an airship attack at the time.

The German army Zeppelins were squandered in reconnaissance flights over the battle-front where their huge bulk offered easy targets for ground fire. Three were lost within a month of the outbreak of war. The survivors were withdrawn by a badly shaken German High Command and, slowly, the Navy began to emerge as the champion of the Zeppelin. Under Korvetten-Kapitän Peter Strasser the Naval Airship Division developed as an élite force.

Strasser was determined to make the new service 'aggressively efficient'. He put all of his dynamic energy into the training of hand-picked crews, and agitated for more and better Zeppelins to be built. He made it his duty to accompany his men on all operational flights, and near the end of the war lost his life when the L70 was shot down into the North Sea on August 6th, 1918.

Strasser began preparing airship bases along the North Sea coast of Germany. Sheds were built, or commenced, at Tondern in Frisia, Fuhlsbüttel near Hamburg, and at Nordholz on the mouth of the river Elbe. The latter was an amazing shed built on a turntable so the doors could be turned into wind to ease handling of the huge unwieldy airships. The new Zeppelins he had requested were slowly taking shape at Friedrichshafen and until they were ready he concentrated on training crews and preparing for 'Der Tag' when the order to attack London would be given.

Similarly the German army was preparing bases in Belgium at Etterbeek, Maubeuge, Berchem Ste Agathe, Evere, Gontrode and Cognelée. There was little co-operation between the two services and they were competing to be first over London.

In England on the outbreak of war Winston Churchill's 'swarm of hornets' comprised a handful of guns, of debatable value, and a motley collection of stick-and-string aircraft, most incapable of carrying any armament! But sitting, passively, waiting for the Zeppelins to come was not part of his scheme. Churchill firmly believed that attack was the best form of defence, and the RNAS squadron at Dunkirk was ordered to attack the German Army's airship sheds at Düsseldorf and Cologne.

Two tiny single-seat Sopwith Tabloids were prepared and moved to an advance airfield at Antwerp; they were to be piloted by Squadron Commander Spenser Grey and Flight Lieutenant R L G Marix. Marix took off for Düsseldorf at 1.30pm on

A typical Sopwith Tabloid, No 1208 at Great Yarmouth Air Station.

October 8th 1914. He reached the sheds and dropped his two 20lb bombs. The attack was astonishingly successful, as Marix was later to report. 'As I pulled out of my dive I looked over my shoulder and was rewarded with the sight of enormous sheets of flame pouring out of the shed. It was a magnificent sight.' The new Zeppelin ZIX was totally destroyed, but only one man, a mechanic on the roof, was killed. The Tabloid did not escape unscathed. Marix was faced with a 110 mile return flight with no rudder control, shrapnel had jammed it in a fore and aft position. He eventually landed some miles north of Antwerp and hitched a lift back to base on a refugee train. Here Marix learned that Spenser Grey had returned safely from Cologne, but in poor visibility had not located the Zeppelin sheds, instead dropping his bombs on the railway station.

Encouraged by the success of the raid on Düsseldorf Churchill made arrangements for a much more ambitious raid, to the Zeppelin factory at Friedrichshafen, where it was known that two Zeppelins were under construction and nearing completion. On October 21st Lieutenant N Pemberton Billing was sent to Belfort, the nearest point in France to the target, where he obtained permission for the Admiralty to use the aerodrome within its fortifications, and prepared detailed plans of the proposed route. At the same time a special squadron was assembled at Manchester. On November 10th four pilots, eleven mechanics and four brand-new 80hp Gnome-engined Avro 504s fitted with special bomb racks, were shipped from Southampton to Le Havre, then conveyed by special train to Belfort. Here they were assembled and, in great secrecy, prepared for the raid. The pilots chosen were Squadron Commander E F Briggs, Flight Commander J T Babington, Flight Lieutenant S V Sippe and Flight Sub-Lieutenant R P Cannon.

On the morning of Saturday November 21st 1914, the four Avros took off, each carrying four 20lb bombs. Cannon's machine failed to rise and broke a tail-skid, but the remaining three climbed safely on the 125 mile flight to Friedrichshafen and reached there about noon. Sippe recorded 'When half a mile from the sheds I put the machine into a dive and came down to 700 feet. Dropped one bomb in enclosure to put gunners off their aim and when in correct position put two into works and shed. The fourth bomb failed to release .... flew north out of range of guns, then turned back to waterside shed to try and release it. Fired on again so dived down to surface of lake and made good my escape'. The three pilots succeeded in destroying a Zeppelin in its shed and the gas works, which exploded in flames.

Sippe and Babington returned safely but Briggs' Avro was damaged by ground fire and forced to land near his target. He was captured and imprisoned, but subsequently made a successful escape with a very young army officer, the latter wearing girl's clothes and at suitable moments pretending to be Briggs' sweetheart.

Cheering as the results may have been to the British public the raids did nothing to curb Peter Strasser's impatience to be let loose over London. He now, in December, had a fleet of five Zeppelins ready to strike. Finally on January 9th 1915 the Kaiser gave his permission for Strasser to raid England, but with the stipulation that attacks be 'expressly restricted to military shipyards, arsenals, docks, and in general, military establishments, and that London itself was not to be bombed.'

Ten days after the Kaiser's announcement weather conditions were promising enough for the first raid to set out. Three naval Zeppelins L3 and L4, Kapitänleutnants Johann Fritz and Magnus Graf von Platen Hallermund respectively, from Fuhlsbüttel, and L6, Oberleutnant Horst Freiherr von Buttlar Brandenfels from Nordholz set course for England. L6 was forced to return with engine trouble but L3 and L4 made landfall on the coast of Norfolk.

At 8.30pm L3 dropped nine bombs on Yarmouth, killing two and injuring three civilians, besides wrecking several houses. L4 over north-east Norfolk dropped bombs indiscriminately around King's Lynn, killing one man and one woman and injuring a further 13. Both Zeppelins returned safely from this pioneer raid but less than a month later, on February 17th, they were lost in a snow storm off the coast of Jutland. On March 5th L8 set out from Düsseldorf to raid the east coast but, caught by a North Sea gale, was forced back over Nieuport where Belgian gunners shot her down.

Although frustrating to the defenders, who were learning by bitter experience the overwhelming difficulty of destroying these monsters, or even preventing their attacks, the Zeppelins were also encountering problems, especially with navigation, that only time and experience would cure. The main difficulty, much to Strasser's disillusionment, was that the early naval Zeppelins had insufficient range to reach London. Strasser saw the prize slipping from his grasp; the honour of first over London was to fall to the military Zeppelins based in Belgium, much closer to the British capital.

Building up strength in Belgian lairs the German military Zeppelins were ready to commence raids over England. On March 17th 1915 the new Zeppelin ZXII commanded by Kapitän Ernst Lehmann set out from Maubeuge with a three ton bomb load. Fog over the English coast forced it back, bombing Calais harbour instead. This raid is of interest because it saw the first use of an observation car lowered from the Zeppelin. Thus the airship could remain safely above cloud level and drop bombs on the instructions of the observer, below the clouds. Not that this helped ZXII to reach base safely, for it landed in a railway cutting on its return to Maubeuge and was damaged.

During April the naval Zeppelins continued hit and run raids sporadically over the East coast, as far north as Tyneside, then on the 29th the Army Airship Service made its first successful attack. Hauptmann Erich Linnarz, commanding the brand new LZ38, crossed the coast at Felixstowe and dropped bombs on Ipswich and Bury St Edmunds before making for home under cover of fog. Although six houses were burnt out there were no casualties. The RNAS were not slow to send up patrols in search of the raiders, but poor visibility regularly forced their return, after a fruitless hunt, to face the hazards of a night landing.

Linnarz was back on May 10th, arriving over the coast near Southend at 2.45am. The airship dropped an incendiary beside the *Royal Edward*, an old hulk employed as a prisoner of war ship. His countrymen aboard were not at all enthusiastic about Linnarz's latest sortie. While over Southend between 90 and 100 bombs were dropped, killing one woman and injuring two men. A house and timber yard were destroyed by fire, and several more houses damaged. Linnarz now turned inland but ran into heavy anti-aircraft fire from some new guns at Cliffe near Canvey Island. His command damaged, he turned back towards Belgium.

Although lionized and given the hero treatment in Berlin, Linnarz was something of a martinet, having been at one time an instructor at Charlottenburg Military Academy. He was so enraged at this hostile reception that, after turning back, he seized a piece of card and angrily scrawled in blue pencil: 'You English. We have come and will come again. Kill or cure. German.' The card was thrust into a weighted message streamer and dropped over the side. It was recoved from the mud flats at Canvey Island later that morning.

Linnarz, and LZ38, came again in the early hours of May 17th, dropping bombs between Margate and Dover where the Zeppelin was illuminated by searchlights. Not liking to be in the limelight in quite this fashion Linnarz took his command north, to the Goodwin Sands, and thence back to Belgium with the approach of dawn.

Unbeknown to him, Linnarz had one visitor on his flight across England. Up from Westgate airfield in an Avro 504C, armed with two incendiary bombs and two grenades, was Flight Sub-Lieutenant R H Mulock. Canadian born Mulock was previously reputed to have said to his CO 'There's no use trying to swat a wasp with a wisp of straw. You need to get a kettle of boiling water, pour it down their hole and scuttle the blasted lot. That's what we have to do, blast the bastards in their sheds!' He now found himself chasing the Zeppelin over Oxney, but at that moment the giant airship climbed rapidly away from the tiny Avro and Mulock had to return, frustrated once more, to Westgate.

While LZ38 was cruising over the English countryside two other Zeppelins were spending the night along the French coast. These were LZ37 and LZ39. Details of their movements were sent to St Pol airfield. At 3.15am LZ39 was dimly seen against a sky faintly streaked by the light of the approaching dawn, but soon lost in the morning mists. All available machines were sent up in pursuit, among them Squadron Commander Spenser Grey in a single-seat Nieuport and Flight Sub-

Lieutenant Rex Warneford, also in a Nieuport, with Leading Mechanic G E Meddis as observer. At 3.30am LZ39 was spotted making for Ostend, Grey and Warneford attacked the giant airship from below with machine-gun and rifle fire. The Zeppelin disdainfully put her nose up and climbed away from her attackers.

Flight Commander A W Bigsworth in Avro 504 No 1009, encountered LZ39 at 10,000ft over Ostend. He succeeded in climbing 200ft above the Zeppelin and, passing over from stem to bow, he dropped four 20lb bombs along her back. Owing to heavy German 'archie' he was forced to break off the combat and watched the airship trailing smoke in the direction of Evere. It made a safe but rough landing at the shed with one dead officer and some wounded men. An inspection revealed five damaged gas bags and the loss of the starboard after propeller.

Flt Cdr A W Bigsworth poses in front of Avro 504, No 1009 in which he damaged LZ39 on the morning of May 17, 1915. The bomb racks are just visible beneath the fuselage.

Both sides had much to think about following the events of May 17th 1915. The Zeppelin commanders could no longer afford to be contemptuous of the British defences, the old Lion's cubs had sharp teeth. But intercepting the airships was no sinecure either. Large targets they might be, but remarkably nimble and difficult to locate in the dark. It would clearly need a skilful pilot, with a large measure of luck, to bring one of the leviathans down.

Artists' impression of a Zeppelin raid over London.

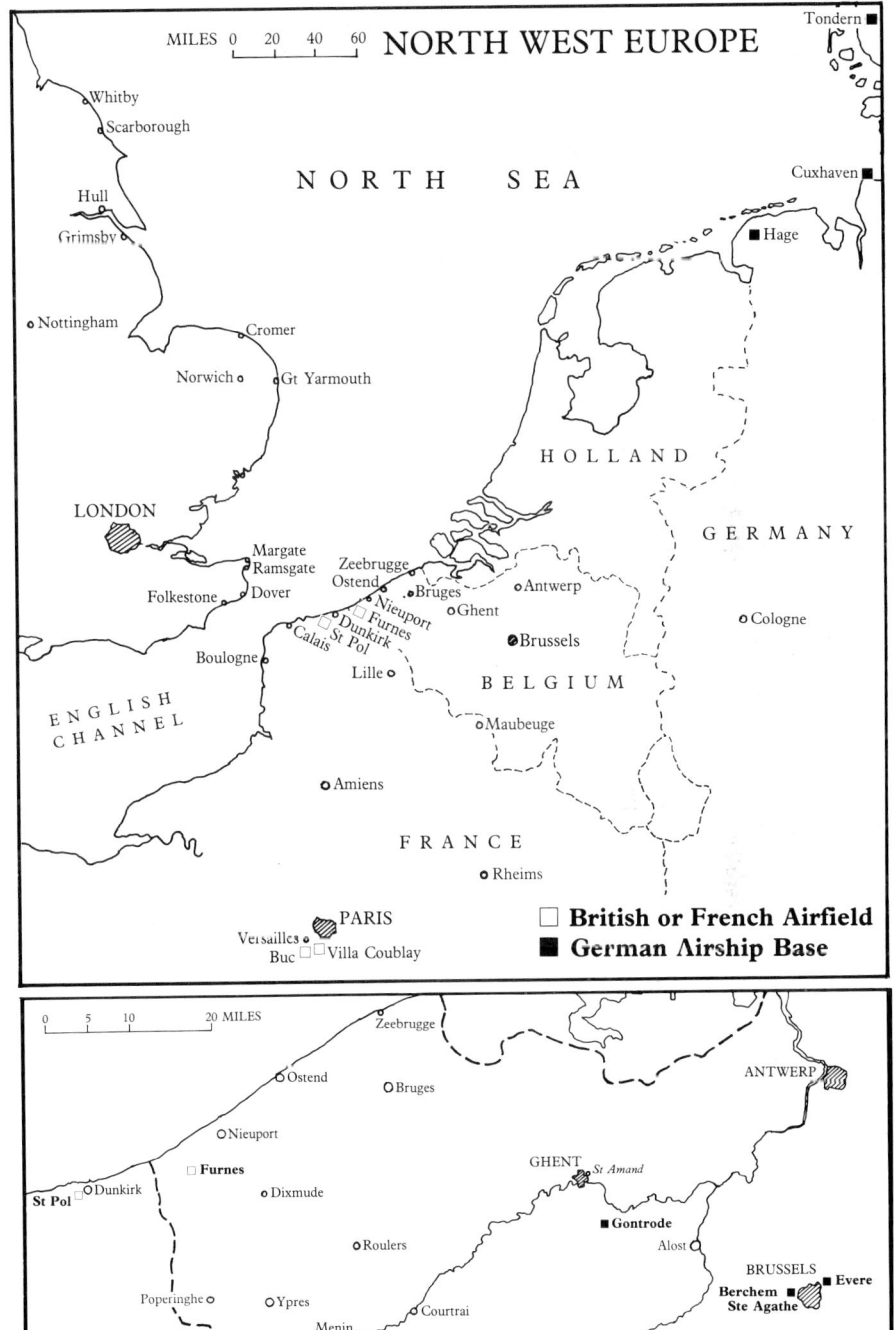

MILES 0 20 40 60 **NORTH WEST EUROPE**

Tondern ■

○Whitby

○Scarborough

N O R T H   S E A

Cuxhaven ■

Hull

Grimsby ○

■Hage

○Nottingham

○Cromer

Norwich ○   ○Gt Yarmouth

H O L L A N D

G E R M A N Y

LONDON

Margate
Ramsgate
Ostend
Folkestone ○Dover

Zeebrugge
□ Nieuport
Furnes
Dunkirk
St Pol
Calais

●Bruges

○Antwerp
○Ghent

●Brussels

○Cologne

Boulogne ○

○Lille

B E L G I U M

E N G L I S H
C H A N N E L

○Maubeuge

○Amiens

F R A N C E

○Rheims

Versailles ○ PARIS
Buc □□Villa Coublay

□ **British or French Airfield**
■ **German Airship Base**

0   5   10   20 MILES

Zeebrugge

○Ostend   ○Bruges

ANTWERP

○Nieuport

□ **Furnes**

GHENT
○ *St Amand*

St Pol □
○Dunkirk

○Dixmude

■ **Gontrode**

Alost ○

○Roulers

BRUSSELS   ■ **Evere**
Berchem
Ste Agathe

Poperinghe ○   ○Ypres

○Courtrai

Menin ○

77

12

Fire over England

By May 31st 1915 everything was ready for the first air raid on London. The Kaiser, enraged by an air attack on his headquarters at Charleville, which he considered a personal insult from one monarch to another, had given his permission for air raids on the enemy capital, though he still insisted on strategic targets only: historic buildings, royal residences and the homes of the poor should be spared. It was not until July 20th that permission was given for raids on the city without discrimination, but Zeppelin navigation and bomb-aiming were rarely so accurate, and hits and misses were largely a matter of luck.

The first airship to make an attack on London was none other than LZ38 with Hauptmann Linnarz, operating from Evere in Belgium and making use of his previous experience to reach his target without being detected.

'I searched for a cloud behind which we could slip through the English coastal defences,' Linnarz said later, when describing the attack for neutral reporters in Germany. 'Under us, on the shimmering sea, cruised the enemy patrol boats. I prudently ordered the lights out. In the control car, the only illumination was on the dial of the machine telegraph. In his narrow cubicle the radio-operator sat with his headset over his ears, listening to the confusion of signals and voices whispering in the infinity of space ...'*

Then they recognised the outline of the coast ahead of them. 'Suddenly,' said Linnarz, 'we had a queer feeling as if our nerves were tightening in an almost joyous anticipation. Would we succeed in breaking through the chain of coastal batteries and remaining unobserved or at least undamaged?'*

The LZ38 reached the mouth of the Thames about 10.00, in fine weather with a light north to north-west wind. The moon was not due to rise for over an hour. The airship was first sighted over Margate where she was met with machine-gun fire that had no effect because of the height at which she was flying. Linnarz then steered across to the Essex shore of the estuary and followed a curving course inland from Shoeburyness, over Billericay and Brentwood, until he arrived above London and began this first attack on the capital by dropping bombs on Stoke Newington about 11.20pm. His course then passed in a loop over Hoxton, Shoreditch, Whitechapel, Stepney, West Ham and Leytonstone, and a total of 30 grenades and 90 incendiary bombs were dropped, a total of about one ton of bombs.

During this time the airship was unseen and almost unheard, which only added to

Monsters of the Purple Twilight by Ernest Dudley, p44, 46; Harrap, 1960

78

the fear and uncertainty on the ground, because of the great height maintained throughout the raid, and the London guns, later to become an extensive and well-organized deterrent to raiders, were not even brought into action. Linnarz then left England on a more northerly course, passing over the mouth of the Crouch at 12.30, and returned to his base in triumph.

For the people of London, the raid had brought the first realization of possible disaster. What they had known in theory since Blériot crossed the Channel in 1909, that Britain was no longer an island, was now being seen in practice. Civilians and their homes were no longer safe simply because they were far away from the front lines: seven people killed, 35 injured (including women and children), and numerous homes damaged by explosion and fire, were, as everyone realized, only a foretaste of things to come.

At this point official policy on newspaper reporting of raids in Britain was abruptly changed, even before Linnarz and the LZ38 had left the country. Instead of the circumstantial accounts which had made it quite clear how little damage had been done by the earlier raids, and which had therefore tended to discredit the airship as a weapon even in Germany, only the briefest reports were now to be permitted.

The Admiralty issued instructions to the press that the exact localities affected, especially in the London area, were not to be named, nor the observed course of airships described or shown on a map. Casualties could be ennumerated, but only minimum descriptions of damage given.

This was of course intended to deprive the enemy of what had previously been a useful source of information, enabling them to check not only the effect of their attacks but also the accuracy of their navigation. Buttlar Brandenfels even admitted in his memoirs to having left a blank in one of his reports until the arrival of English newspapers should enable him to fill in the name of the town on which his bombs had fallen.

Once this knowledge was denied, the Germans were never fully aware either of the errors, often extreme, in their navigation, or of the chronic unreliability of their radio-bearing system. Bombs which might have done serious damage were therefore sometimes dropped on open countryside, or even into the sea, by Zeppelin commanders whose confidence in the knowledge of their course or position was entirely misplaced.

On the other hand, there was now no authoritative contradiction of German claims concerning the success of their raids, and even when these claims were exaggerated they were now more widely believed than before, as press silence was taken for confirmation.

A full inquest was held on the three adults and four children who died either in the raid or later from their injuries. During the proceedings a Lieutenant Cobett, called as an expert witness, said that a label had been found showing that the incendiary bombs had been made at Krupp's works at Essen. These bombs had handles on the top, and it might be useful for the public to know that they could be thrown out of the window with a pair of tongs or a strong stick before they could set a place on fire.

The jury brought in a verdict that the victims had been murdered by a hostile force, but the Coroner said that he did not think there was anything to be gained from a verdict of murder, even though, from a moral point of view, it was murder of a most despicable kind. He therefore advised the jury to bring in a verdict that the deceased had died of injuries received from bombs dropped by hostile aircraft.

Colonel A Rawlinson, soon to play a leading part in the development of London's defences, observed that to him, freshly returned from France, the LZ38's bombs seemed inefficient and the material damage negligible, but he could also see that the moral impact was much greater, and by no means such as the Germans had long anticipated and indeed continued to expect throughout most of the war. True, there was fear, even panic: people who could afford to leave London and live elsewhere did so; and there was a great upsurge of fury against the 'baby-killers', but these reactions did not lead to the rapid demoralization that was looked for. Instead, recruitment to the armed forces increased, as an expression of the feelings of fury, while fear brought pressure to bear on the authorities to defend the city effectively, and this in fact was done with remarkable speed once the raid had exposed London's true state of unpreparedness.

If such guns as were available to defend the capital on May 31st remained silent, no fewer than nine aircraft went up in pursuit of the raider, but only one pilot, Flight Lieutenant A W Robertson, flying a Blériot from Rochford, even saw the LZ38, which was high above him as he reached 6,000 feet, and he was compelled to land with engine failure before he could try to intercept her.

Also seeking the LZ38 that night was Warren Merriam, who had earlier received the honour of having his hand trodden on by Winston Churchill while the air-minded politician was stepping from Merriam's aircraft during an inspection at Hendon. Merriam and his observer, Sub-Lieutenant J S Morrison, had even less luck than Robertson: 'We received instructions that, should we encounter a Zeppelin and fail to destroy it with our rifles and hand grenades, we were to ram it! ...when the alarm finally came through we took off in a thick ground mist and flew over central London. There we cruised for about two hours without seeing a sign of a "gas-bag" anywhere. At the end of these two hours the light on my dashboard failed and I was unable to read any of my instruments ... Seeing the faint outline of the Thames below, and taking a rough bearing from the stars, I headed back in the general direction of the aerodrome. Goodness knows how I ever reached it ... my goggles oiled up, and as I reached up to wipe them they flew off ... [but] we landed like a duck on a pond, slightly bending the axle, but otherwise safely'.*

In fact all the attempts to intercept the LZ38 that night revealed the difficulties under which aircraft of the period laboured when opposed to airships, especially at night: Flight Commander W P de Courcy Ireland, flying a Short S81 seaplane from Great Yarmouth, had difficulty taking off with only four 16 pound bombs as armament; he failed to sight the enemy, and on returning to find Great Yarmouth hidden in mist had to crash-land in a field nearby, still holding the bombs on his lap.

The LZ38 even managed to claim a victim among the airborne defenders although they did not meet. Flight Lieutenant D M Barnes left Hendon in a Sopwith Gunbus pusher biplane with Flight Sub-Lieutenant Ben Travers as his

*First Through the Clouds p102/3; B T Batsford, 1954

observer: they managed to reach an altitude of 5,000 feet, too low to encounter the airship, but too high for the Sopwith, which suffered engine failure and crashed in a field at Hatfield, killing Barnes outright and injuring Travers who was fortunately thrown clear of the deadly weight of the rear-mounted engine.

These incidents were typical of the adventures and disasters encountered by London's defenders, who like the civilians and even the attackers themselves were venturing into the unknown of total warfare. After one raid, by one airship, on a great capital city, everyone could still only guess at what aerial bombardment might eventually achieve. The number of casualties inflicted in Britain, less than 2,000 by the end of the war, and the material damage done, were insignificant compared to the lives lost and the destruction in the battle zones of Europe, but the disruption of the daily life and work of the nation took its toll psychologically and in other ways, and it has been estimated that munitions production alone was reduced by as much as one sixth as a result of air raids.

Germany's 'night of terror', so carefully planned and so long awaited with apprehension, was a strange paradox: ineffectual in itself, yet full of significance for the future. Hauptmann Linnarz's citation for his Iron Cross might truthfully have contained the words 'from today there are no more non-combatants' and called the children's graves in East London to witness.

A Sopwith Gunbus at Hendon on Home Defence duty, 1915. Only a small number of these pusher biplanes were built by Sopwith and Robey. Powered by a 100hp Gnome rotary engine this Sopwith built machine is fitted with a single Lewis gun.

13

The End of the LZ37

As a result of the LZ38's success over London at the end of May plans were quickly drawn up for more ambitious raids by both naval and military airships on the British capital, but it was pure coincidence rather than combined organization which led the two services to choose the same date for their next attack.

During the afternoon of Sunday June 6th, 1915 Kapitänleutnant Heinrich Mathy in naval Zeppelin L9 left his shed at Hage, north Germany, and set course for the Wash. Then, as the long summer's day faded into night three military airships lifted off from their bases in Belgium. Hauptmann Linnarz, in LZ38, developed engine trouble almost immediately and was forced to land again, his airship being towed back into its shed at Evere. LZ39, with Hauptmann Masius in command, rose from Berchem Ste Agathe to join Oberleutnant von der Haegen in LZ37. The giant Maybach engines gathered speed and their humming increased to a roar as both gained height safely and headed north-west towards the coast from where they would plot their route to London.

Between Ostend and Zeebrugge there were two lighthouses, by which the German navigators fixed their course for England. These lighthouses were equipped with mechanisms which enabled their keepers to direct beams of light vertically into the sky, and airships steering due west between them would eventually arrive at the mouth of the River Thames.

Half-way across the Dover Straits the south-westerly wind freshened, bringing with it a thick fog which swiftly engulfed the two airships, completely blotting out their view of the coasts below and eliminating all hope of finding their target as they struggled to hold course. The wind and fog also prevented Mathy in L9 from reaching London in the time available, so using the wind he headed north over the Humber towards Flamborough Head, then turned about as he caught sight of the lights of Hull below through the drifting mists.

He reached the city about 12.30am and, after dropping illuminating parachute flares, proceeded to bomb the harbour area from 5000 feet. He was fired upon by HMS *Adventure* which happened to be in dry dock for repairs, so he promptly rose to 6,500 feet out of range of her guns. As the city had no proper anti-aircraft protection Mathy continued to drop bombs and incendiaries over the area for some 20 minutes. During this time he totally destroyed 40 houses and shops, killed 24 and injured another 40 people, burnt out a sawmill and caused much serious damage. L9 then made for Grimsby and released another seven incendiary bombs,

A Henry Farman F27 and a Nieuport 12, possibly at St Pol. The F27, which had a metal structure, was used by Wilson and Mills to bomb Evere. About 60 were ordered for use by the RNAS.

which did little damage, before continuing down the Humber. The guns at Immingham and Waltham fired a few shots as she passed overhead, but fog around the mouth of the river prevented any aircraft from taking off in pursuit and the airship disappeared into the night on her way back to Hage.

Meanwhile, without even crossing the English coast, LZ37 and LZ39 had reluctantly turned about and were making their way back to Belgium, unaware that their radio signals had been picked up and relayed to the Admiralty in London. Wing Commander Arthur Longmore, in charge of No 1 Squadron RNAS at St Pol, related: '...they were reported to me over the direct telephone line from the Admiralty as being on their way back. I sent off Warneford and Rose on their Moranes to intercept in the vicinity of Ghent, and Wilson and Mills in their big weight-carrying Henry Farmans to bomb the Zeppelin sheds at Evere, near Brussels. I hoped by this arrangement to catch one or more Zeppelins in the air, or, failing that, to set them alight after they had returned to their sheds.'[*] If the two Moranes failed to catch sight of the returning airships they were to head south and unload their bombs on the sheds at Berchem Ste Agathe, to the west of Brussels.

At 12.40am on June 7th Flight Lieutenant J P Wilson[**] took off into the mists on his Henry Farman biplane, followed after a short interval by Flight Sub-Lieutenant J S Mills.[***] At 2.05am Wilson arrived over Evere and was immediately picked up in the beam of a searchlight which appeared to be flashing a signal to him from the landing field. He promptly replied with short flashes from his pocket torch, and was relieved to see the light go out. For the next fifteen minutes he circled the area, without being fired at from the ground, as he strained his eyes to discern the outline of the large shed. As the sky brightened Wilson pinpointed his target and from

[*] *From Sea to Sky* p45; Geoffrey Bles, 1946
[**] John Philip Wilson, DFC, AFC 1889-1959. Played cricket for Yorkshire 1911-13. RNAS commission, August 1914. Retired on medical grounds 1919 with only six months life expectancy but recovered to become a well-known amateur steeplechase jockey in the 1920s. Re-enlisted in 1940 for non-flying duties and left the service in 1944 to work with the International Relief Organisation in Germany until 1947.
[***] John Stanley Mills, b.1889. Awarded pilot's certificate Jan 26th, 1915.

2000ft released his three 65lb bombs, the second of which caused a large explosion and filled the air with clouds of black smoke. As Mills arrived over the shed the ground defences opened up and he was forced to take evasive action, so he climbed to 5000ft before dropping his bombs. As the two aircraft departed into the mist the sky behind them was suddenly lit with the glare of intense fire — they had destroyed not only a shed, but LZ38, the first of the London raiders!

About the same time as the two Henry Farmans had taken off for this raid the bomb-laden Moranes were being prepared on the Belgian aerodrome at Furnes, some 15 miles east of St Pol, which was occupied by a French squadron but was also used by individual RNAS pilots as an advance landing ground during their offensive work along the Belgian coast. There Rex and his companion, Sub-Lieutenant Rose, clambered into their frail machines and pulled down their goggles. The propellers were swung, the engines primed, and the two 80hp rotary engines spluttered into life. The smell of burnt castor oil filled the cockpit as Rex peered in to check his instruments, noting the time was 1.00am then, with a wave to the mechanics to release his machine, they were off.

Two Morane-Saulnier Parasols at St Pol, with Rex's 3253 on the right. Neither carry armament, but both are fitted with similar bomb racks.

The two aircraft climbed hesitantly into the cold night air, the lights of the runway flares quickly disappearing as they rose into the swathes of mist. They soon got separated, and by the time Rex had broken through the top of the mist layers there was no sign of his companion. In fact Rose had lost his way in the dark because his instruments lights failed, and he was forced to land in a field near Cassel. He overturned his Morane in the process but climbed out unhurt.

Rex was now on his own, heading east over Dixmude where he had previously attacked the long-range gun, when he suddenly caught sight of a pencil slim grey shape far north beyond Ostend. In an instant it had vanished from sight — a ghostly apparition or just imagination? He pushed up his goggles and rubbed his eyes. His nerves tingled with tension and an involuntary shiver ran down his back. He banked north-east towards the vision: there it was again, right in front of him, an airship indeed, silvered by the moon, floating dreamlike towards its base.

It was about 20 miles off and heading south-east, as Rex set off in pursuit. For the next 45 minutes as their courses converged he watched it tensely, sometimes losing sight of it for a few minutes through billowing layers of mist, as he climbed steadily to a height where he could run in from behind and drop his bombs. A few miles south of Bruges Rex finally turned into position to attack. As he did so he suddenly saw flashes from the airship: bullets whined past his machine and — all hope of surprise gone — he pulled back the stick and the Morane banked steeply up and out of range.

Aboard the Zeppelin there was sudden apprehension at the sound of gunfire. Oberleutnant von der Haegen and his crew had been concentrating on getting LZ37 safely home against the gusting wind, so it came as a surprise when the top observer gunner reported opening fire at this unexpected raider. Orders were instantly given: to the gunner 'Hold Fire'; to the crew 'Release ballast', and to the coxswain 'Trim and ascend.' The airship tilted and rose rapidly. The top gunner's voice came down the speaking-tube again: 'Aeroplane in sight, now only 800 metres astern.' The commander's clipped voice replied calmly 'Open fire when in range.' There was a short respite, then the gunner's voice, sharply 'I engage enemy aeroplane.'

As Rex retreated out of range of the Zeppelin's guns, von der Haegen turned to his navigating officer and said, 'See, the Englander is frightened of us. We will give him some of his own medicine. We will show him that we are not to be threatened

The 1925 Grand National winner, J P Wilson on Double Chance.

The only known photographs of LZ37, showing the early open boat shaped control cars. A gunners' platform is just visible on top of the envelope forward. Although similar in many respects to 'Viktoria Luise' it was larger and had simplified tail surfaces.

by a midge.' He gave orders to the coxswain who obediently swung the wheel and altered course to port, allowing the airship's gunners a clear field of fire. It was a foolhardy decision, born of the overbearing arrogance of her commander. Almost immediately the Morane swooped in to attack again and was swept by a rain of bullets, but miraculously received no mortal wound and swerved away upwards for another try.

Once more von der Haegen urgently gave the order to release ballast. Once again the airship responded sluggishly as it ascended. For a brief time the duel became a stalemate. Rex told Lieutenant Marsden afterwards, 'After several attempts to get above him again, I came to the conclusion that the best thing I could do was to try and make him think that I had chucked the game and was going home.' So he headed off to the west, well astern of the Zeppelin, and once out of range the firing ceased.

Although the Morane possessed superior speed its slow rate of climb and lack of armament robbed it of complete fighting superiority. Rex knew that from now on he must be cautious, and do nothing that might provoke the German commander into giving further orders to release ballast, so he decided to play a waiting game and remained well astern, watching how the Zeppelin would make its next move.

By 2.15am the airship was north of Ghent, still heading east at 10,000 feet, and it puzzled the coxswain why his commander had not altered course for their base. Almost as though von der Haegen had read his thoughts he gave orders to run for the shed at Gontrode. He was uncertain whether he had really shaken off his assailant, but he felt that as he neared the sanctuary of his base the aircraft could be lured into range of the anti-aircraft gun batteries around the shed.

Rex was also wondering how long this stalemate could continue, as he was not sure if his fuel would last much longer, when he became aware of the Zeppelin gradually turning south and dipping its nose. This was it. He could not afford to wait any longer. He pulled back the stick and the Morane climbed to 11,000 feet, steadily closing the gap between the two aircraft.

Dawn was breaking: the short summer night was almost over. Far below the city of Ghent lay in semi-darkness, partly hidden by the morning mist which was beginning to rise up into the air and swirl around the descending airship. Rex could see that the gunners would soon be unable to pick him out as he made his attack.

He eased the stick forward. Down he came in his final dive, engine switched off so that no sound louder than the whistling of the wind around the Morane should announce his approach. He came sweeping round towards the stern of the Zeppelin at full speed from a towering height. Rex watched the broad green back drawing closer and closer as he calculated the right moment to release his bombs. He was concentrating so hard that he did not even notice the gun-platform on top of the airship at the bow, and no one on board could see him as they peered into the wreaths of mist, but at the last moment the unmistakable whine of the diving aircraft penetrated their consciousness, and they sensed that danger was near.

One hundred and fifty feet above the seemingly heedless monster Rex released the first of his bombs. He later said: 'At that time I thought that it had no effect. I loosed another, but the third definitely did the trick, and I pulled off the remaining three automatically, almost unconsciously.'

A typical artist's impression of the exploit as portrayed in the press. Due to lack of information most publications showed the aircraft as the better known Blériot type.

The result was a terrific explosion which almost tore the Zeppelin in two: it was instantly engulfed in flames. The blazing envelope, borne up in the air by hot gases, maintained height for a while but slowly disintegrated. Great banners of flame sprang through rents in the fabric and flew upwards, causing currents of hot air to swirl past the Morane, which, caught in the wild vortex, was turned over and over. For a time the machine flew upside down, with Rex hanging in the safety harness. When at last his aircraft regained its equilibrium he saw the Zeppelin floating down to earth like a gigantic torch. He told Marsden: 'I looked down and watched it burning. I had the strangest feeling of detached curiosity, almost as though its death agonies had nothing to do with me.'

He was brought back to reality by the danger of his own situation and the realization that there was no petrol in his tank. He did not at once understand what could have happened to it and ruefully concluded that it must have been lost 'as the aeroplane was somersaulting.'

There was nothing for it now but a forced landing in enemy territory. He did not anticipate a very pleasant reception should he be captured. As he glided down, the sound of further explosions came to his ears. The Zeppelin must have reached the ground.

The German coxswain who survived the wreck told what had been happening on board the airship: 'The men in the forward control car were the first to feel the great shudder of the impact and explosion. Above us the vast envelope quivered and began to wrinkle and collapse. The wheel went dead in my hand, and the gondola trembled. All around were shouts and confused orders; we were encompassed by an increasing and terrible heat. I saw dark shapes of men silhouetted against a ruddy glow as their flailing arms tried to protect their faces. Some of them climbed over the sides of the car and flung themselves into space. I could not make myself let go of the wheel. I clung to it like a drowning man until it broke in my hands. I was flung to the floor. The scorching heat increased and increased, and our clothes burst into flames.

The gondola began to tilt and rock until, with a terrible sound of breaking wood and metal it tore away from the main structure and plunged towards the ground. I knew no more until I woke up in hospital and found out that I was the only survivor.'

Rex had no idea where the Zeppelin had fallen, and later was shocked to learn that it had landed on a large convent, killing and injuring nuns and children.

The convent of St Elisabeth, in the Mont St Amand district of Ghent, formed a little township on its own, inhabited by about seven hundred members and totally enclosed by high walls and a moat. The Order was founded in 1240, and the nuns belonging to the community, conspicuous for their wide white winged headdresses, devoted themselves not only to the religious life but also to works of charity. At the time of the disaster they were sheltering refugees as well as the children of their orphanage. The Béguinage houses were nearly all two storeys high, mainly gothic in character, and there were eight of them, surrounded by their orchards and gardens, with their little church forming the centre of the whole.

The burning mass of the Zeppelin fell near the middle of the block. Terrible scenes were enacted: many of the crew were already dead, and their scorched and

Oberleutnant Otto von der Haegen, 1887-1915. Captain of the Zeppelin LZ37.

dismembered bodies were flung about in all directions. The convent caught fire, and in the blaze two nuns and a child perished. A man lost his life attempting rescue, and another, in a fruitless attempt to save a child, fell from a second floor window and broke both his legs.

Contemporary reports stated that there were 28 people on board the Zeppelin,* including engineers from the factory who were making a trip for experimental purposes, so the loss of this ship was doubly disastrous for the Germans. Certainly all but one of this crew died, either in the crash or soon afterwards, and by noon the only one left alive was *Steuermann* (coxswain) Alfred Mühler who recovered and returned to the airship service, and who had his description of events on board the LZ37 published many years later.

Eyewitnesses declared that he fell from the burning gondola from an altitude of no more than 100 feet. He landed on the roof of one of the convent buildings and crashed through a skylight into an attic where his fall was broken by a feather bed. He escaped with severe burns, cuts, bruises and shock.

A nun who was a novice at the convent at the time later wrote her own description of the disaster: 'It was on Corpus Christi, and the day of our annual procession. In the afternoon the Blessed Sacrament was carried along the paths of the gardens of our Convent of St Elisabeth, followed by 100 of our sisters and 60 children. The children were dressed in white and carried nosegays of flowers. It was a beautiful day, one of the warmest. There was hardly a cloud in the sky, and larks were singing in the meadows down by the canals. It was to be a day of devotion and heavenly peace.

'Later on the children enjoyed a special tea, and the long tables were decorated with flowers. For a few hours we could forget the cruel war, and our country being occupied by the Germans. Later when the children were in bed, mists began to rise and the wind began to blow. One of our sisters called to me, "Look up in the sky!" And there we could see a great airship. We all knew that she was on her way to drop bombs on some town. She came from the east, and passed quite low over our convent, taking a direction to the west. Later that night the weather changed. The doors were banging and we had to close the windows. Always, we had to black out all our lights. I could not sleep for the sound of the wind, and before morning light I arose early to go to the chapel.

'I met the other sisters, and together we filed down the stairs into the garden. We were about to cross over when we heard a great explosion. We looked up into the sky and could see a Zeppelin in flames drifting towards our convent. We were terribly afraid that it would fall on us. It came nearer and nearer. The sound of its burning was terrible. There were screams, and pieces of metal began to fall all around. Our big bell began to ring its warning for fire. Sisters and the refugees came running out.

'We went back to the dormitory wing where the children were sleeping. They were all awake, and we told them to come out quickly into the garden. Part of this building was on fire. We tried to go back into the orphanage where the little children lived: this too was in flames. We were beaten back, but got inside by a back

*German sources list only nine crew-members killed and one survivor. This was the first army Zeppelin crew to be lost in action.

way, and managed to get most of the children to safety. In the orphanage one little girl lay dead. The others were very brave. There was no panic. Everyone was helping.

'Our Mother Superior assembled us all in the hall of the main building, which was further away from the disaster. She demanded a roll-call, and found that some were missing. We later had to leave this building, as there was a danger that it might also catch fire. When we crossed the garden, a terrible sight met our eyes. It is still impossible for me to recall it without horror, even after all these years.

'The fires which were now all around us made it as light as day. The bodies of dead and dying airmen lay scattered about in their charred uniforms. Some were still alive and groaning terribly. But we were not permitted to go near them, by the German soldiers and police who had arrived from the town. Our chaplain asked if he might give the last rites to the dying, but even he was not allowed to go near. We were all marshalled together and sent to the furthest building. Another roll-call was given and still some were missing. We implored the soldiers to allow us to return to the Béguinage to look for them, but we were not allowed. The soldiers said they would make the search themselves. They found two of our young sisters alive, another unconscious. When they brought them to us they said that two others were dead. One of these was only 15 years of age, we called her our 'little sunshine sister' because she was always happy and laughing. It was not until the next afternoon that her body was recovered. She had fallen through the floor into a downstairs classroom.

Wreckage of the LZ37 in the courtyard of the Convent of St Elisabeth, Ghent.

'Many of our sisters and some of the refugees were burned or injured that night, and part of our convent was in ruins. All the nearby streets of Mont St Amand were closed by the military, and inhabitants ordered to keep inside their houses. But in spite of the German Polizei, many were curious to see the wreck of the Zeppelin and managed to creep out.

'For ourselves and the children we had to find other accommodation within our walls for a long time. One of our sisters tried to take a photograph of the wreck of the airship but the officer on guard came up behind her and took away her camera. Later it was returned to her but without the film.

'On Tuesday morning we were allowed to arrange for the burial of our dead. The service was held in our chapel which was not damaged, although all over the church yard lay pieces of wreckage, and everywhere was the smell of burning and smoke. Nothing was allowed to be moved except by the military, who were about all the time in great numbers. Later 20 large drays, drawn by four horses apiece, took two weeks to clear away the remains of the airship.

'On Wednesday we were permitted to hold another service for the final interment of the dead. As many of us as were able attended and followed the coffins in procession. In the afternoon of the same day, General von Westdorp and his aide came to our Reverend Mother and expressed sorrow for what had happened. He also requested that he and some of his staff might attend the funeral, but she told them that it had already taken place. The next day they sent beautiful wreaths of white flowers for the graves. It seemed that the Germans were not without heart after all.

'In spite of our mourning, there was in all our hearts a fierce joy for the intrepid daring and victory of Lieutenant Warneford. After the war a plaque was fixed on to the wall of our convent in memory of the young airman, and a nearby street had been named after him.

'I am Flemish, and I find it difficult to give the same strength to my descriptions of the events that I would like, in a strange language.'

Mother Thérèse Marguerite.

Commemorative plaque, in French and Flemish, on the convent wall at Ghent.

14

Mission Accomplished

Rex sat reeling in his cockpit, as the Morane glided down through the mist. The conflict with the Zeppelin seemed like a nightmare, fading at dawn. He found himself wondering vaguely where he was going to land, and what would happen to him when he did. He heard one or two dull explosions far away, but all trace of the burning airship had vanished, and everything was blanketed in the wet dripping opaque fog which blinded him. Suddenly the ground rose up at him, and the Morane lurched and creaked as she landed.

As far as Rex could see, which was about the length of his arm, his machine had come to rest on the side of a hill covered with tussocks of rough grass sparkling with dewy spiders' webs. He climbed stiffly out of the cockpit thankful that he was still in one piece. The Morane was standing nearly upright, and did not appear to be damaged. He was surprised to discover that a strange noise somewhere near his face was his own teeth chattering. He was shivering uncontrollably, and felt ravenously hungry. After all the explosions and gunfire this place was as eerily quiet as a tomb. Suddenly the silence was shattered by the sharp barking of a dog. It would be awkward if it awoke someone, who might come outside to see what the noise was about. Fortunately for Rex somebody leaned out of a window and simply cursed the dog, which whined a little, and then subsided.

He gave a sigh of relief, and started to inspect his machine. If he was not able to get her off the ground and fly her back to Allied territory, he would have to destroy her and his papers, so that nothing but his own person could fall into the enemy's hands. It did not take him long to find out the worst of the damage. Apart from a few bullet holes which in themselves would not prevent her from flying the most serious mishap was the broken connection between the pressure and gravity tanks. All the fuel in the main tank had been lost but there was a small quantity left in the reserve tank which might just be sufficient to get him back to behind the English front line.

Spurred on by the unpleasant thought of being taken prisoner he set to work to effect a repair. He had a shrewd idea that the Germans would have guessed that he had been obliged to make a forced landing. By now patrols might have been sent out to search for him. 'My fingers seemed to be all thumbs', he said afterwards, 'and I was always dropping important bits into the long grass, and taking ages to find them', but thanks to his skill with things mechanical, it took him only 15 minutes to repair the joint and reconnect the pipe.

Just as he had finished, a squadron of German cavalry entered the woods on the perimeter of the field, and began energetically quartering every foot of ground in search of him. He heard the squelch and suck of their horses' hooves, and the guttural voices of the soldiers. They sounded so close that it seemed impossible that they would not discover him eventually, but the morning mists were on his side. Though soldiers rode to the very edge of the wood they failed to spot the Morane, and the rattle of their bits and sabres became fainter and fainter as they rode away. Rex knew that this respite could not last. When the mist lifted and the sun came through he was sure to be captured.

'I was not going to leave anything to chance, although I was longing to get on,' he later told Flight Lieutenant Marsden, when he was safely back at the base, 'I religiously doped every one of the cylinders with petrol, by filling an empty Very cartridge cap, and dropping it on to the cylinder heads. Then I swung the prop. Another problem cropped up, for without another chap, I could not keep the engine running long enough for me to get back into the cockpit. After dashing madly from the revolving propeller to the seat in vain, I got another idea. I was pretty desperate by then. I pulled and pushed and bounced her along until I got her nose pointing downhill which was luckily pretty steep. Then I swung the prop. I kept on hauling and pushing her until ... she started to move slowly at first and then as she gathered speed, and I knew she wouldn't stop, I made a leap for the cockpit just as the Boche charged out of the wood firing their carbines in my direction. The old girl responded magnificently as I opened the throttle, and managed to climb out of their range. I could not resist shouting down to them "Give my regards to the Kaiser". I think they only understood the last word, anyway I did not wait for their reply.

'I climbed higher until I cleared the mist. I looked at my petrol gauge and calculated that it would not be very long before I would have to make another forced landing, hoping that this time it would not be in enemy territory. I had to fly low to try and raise some landmark, but soon found myself in the mist; then all at once I saw the shimmer of the sea below — my engine started to splutter and give up, and I just had time to put her down on some short grass before I went over the cliff into the sea. I had no idea where I had landed, until I saw some French soldiers running towards me with their rifles at the ready.

'Out of the frying pan into the fire! Good Lord they were going to shoot me! They rushed up jabbering in their lingo which I could not understand. I tried to assure them I was English and pointed to the identification on the Morane, but they would not have it, and marched me off with my hands up to their commanding officer, who, thank God, could speak English. However he was pretty suspicious, as when he demanded to see my papers I realised that I had destroyed them and was in a fair way to be taken as a spy, who got pretty short shift in those days, especially from the French whose motto was "Shoot first, ask questions afterwards."

'Eventually I half-persuaded them who I was and induced them to contact the aerodromes at St Pol or Furnes who soon reassured them that I was bona fide. After all this had been settled they could not do enough for me, and were full of apologies. All was "entente cordiale" whatever that meant. I was fortified by their cognac, and nearly smothered by their protests of goodwill and salutes on both cheeks. They filled up the Morane's tank, and off I hopped.'

Rex standing by his Morane. The bomb rack fitted to the undercarriage is just visible. This gives a clear impression of the fragility of the aircraft, the only item of substance seeming to be the 80hp Gnome engine, though in fact the engines were often more fragile than the aircraft.

Rex arrived back at St Pol at 10.30am very tired. No one then knew what had happened to him. He made a short report to Wing Commander Longmore and was driven down to the *Empress,* where he rolled into his bunk and slept for eight hours. While he slept the telephone wires were humming from St Pol to Whitehall announcing Rex Warneford's incredible feat of bringing down a Zeppelin single-handed. When he awoke at 7.00pm the news had already flashed around the world.

The first intimation of what had happened came when he was driven back to the airfield where he was greeted by a cheering crowd of pilots and ground staff. He was most embarrassed by this show of appreciation, and bolted into the CO's office to make a more extensive report of the night's work. Senior officers from nearby aerodromes had gathered there and he had to go over the whole of his mission in the greatest detail. He was rather put out by all the fuss. As far as he was concerned he said that killing the Zep was just an ordinary 'op'.

Since the news had reached Whitehall the Government realized that this young man's exploit was the very thing needed to boost the morale of a depressed population. A war that was supposed to end victoriously by Christmas 1914 was dragging into its second year and showed no signs of ending. The sinking of the

Lusitania, coupled with the many enemy advances on the Western front, and the appalling threat of war being brought onto British soil itself by the dreaded air raids and bombing by invincible Zeppelins meant a serious crisis. In this situation Rex's gallant deed, a real life story of David and Goliath, was going to be exploited to the last drop of printer's ink.

The young airman's name, his picture, and the story of the stricken Zeppelin were blazoned across the front pages of every newspaper, and took some of the darkness out of the war's other gloomy bulletins. The story circled the globe while Rex slept exhausted and blissfully ignorant of what Fate had in store for him. Life

THE SPORTSMAN'S BATTALIONS.

ROYAL FUSILIERS.

COLONEL COMMANDING-IN-CHIEF.

OFFICERS COMMANDING THE  KING.

1st BATT.
COLONEL VISCOUNT MAITLAND.

2nd BATT.
COLONEL A. de B. V. PAGET.

HOTEL CECIL,

STRAND, LONDON.

June 8th, 1915.

Sub-Lieut. R.A.J. Warneford, R.N.
   No. 1 Aeroplane Squadron,
      D u n k r i k.
    (C/o Mail Officer, Dover)

Dear Mr. Warneford,

      You cannot think how delighted I was to read of your grand achievement, and how proud to think that you were one of my recruits, and originally belonged to the 2nd. Sportsman's Battalion. The battalions have given you three cheers on your great achievement, and I hope that you will accept the small gold identification disc as a small memento of the short time you belonged to us, and as a souvenir.

      With the best of wishes,

        Yours very sincerely,

        (Mrs) E. Cunliffe-Owen.

BUCKINGHAM PALACE

8th June, 1915.

My dear Balfour,

      If you agree, the King would like
to send the following telegram from him to Flight
Sub-Lieutenant Warneford:-

      "I most heartily congratulate you upon
your splendid achievement of yesterday in which you
single handed destroyed an enemy Zeppelin. I have
much satisfaction in conferring upon you the Victoria
Cross for this gallant act. GEORGE R.I."

      His Majesty feels that if this is to
be sent the sooner the better.

Yours sincerely

Stamfordham

The Rt. Honble.,
   Arthur Balfour, M.P.
     First Lord of the Admiralty.

The swiftest award of a V.C. following an action, and the first to be made by telegram.

would never be the same again, and to the end of his very brief life he would not be able to escape from the merciless glare of publicity.

When his CO told him briefly what lay ahead, he pleaded to be allowed to slip back into the anonymity of his service existence, but Wing Commander Longmore's instructions from the Government were 'To keep Warneford on the ground for as long as his value as propaganda was fully exploited, and until he had returned from London.' From London: at first Rex did not take in what this meant, until he was handed a telegram headed 'Buckingham Palace.' Longmore told him to read it out.

The slip of paper trembled in Rex's hands as he began: 'I most heartily congratulate you upon your splendid achievement of yesterday in which you single handed destroyed an enemy Zeppelin. I have much pleasure in conferring upon you the Victoria Cross for this gallant act. George, R.I.' Slowly the message cleared before his eyes. This was why the CO had mentioned London. But no! he did not want to go there. He did not want any of the crowds and the adulation. He did not want anything else in the world but to go back to the mess on the old *Empress,* which by now he looked on as his home. He wanted to remain on the airfield and take part in the daily 'ops', to tinker about with Fitter Hawkins and his brother on the engines of his beloved Moranes, to fly again; that was what he wanted, what he had dedicated himself to, and where happiness and satisfaction lay.

He looked into the kind eyes of Wing Commander Longmore, but in them he could see no answer to his predicament. 'Sit down' he said, 'take it in slowly, and then let's go into your report again.' He had never sat down in the presence of his CO before. He tried to rearrange his thoughts, and all he could think of was what a long time it seemed since he had taken off to intercept the LZ37; yet it was only 36 hours.

A clerk came into the office with a sheaf of papers, and sat down at a typewriter. To Rex's slow dictation he typed the following:

No.1 Naval Aeroplane Squadron.

8th June, 1915.

Sir,

I have the honour to report as follows:

I left Furnes at 1.00 am on June the 7th on Morane No 3253 under orders to proceed to look for Zeppelins and attack the Berchem St Agathe Airship Shed with six 20 lb bombs.

On arriving at Dixmude at 1.5 am, I observed a Zeppelin apparently over Ostend and proceeded in chase of the same.

I arrived at close quarters a few miles past Bruges at 1.50 am and the Airship opened heavy maxim fire, so I retreated to gain height and the Airship turned and followed me.

At 2.15 am he seemed to stop firing and at 2.25 am I came behind, but well above the Zeppelin; height then 11,000 feet, and switched off my engine to descend on top of him.

When close above him (at 7,000 feet altitude) I dropped my bombs, and, whilst releasing the last, there was an explosion which lifted my machine and turned it over. The aeroplane was out of control for a short period, but went into a nose dive, and the control was regained.

I then saw that the Zeppelin was on the ground in flames and also that there were pieces of something burning in the air all the way down.

The joint on my petrol pipe and pump from the back tank was broken, and at about 2.40 am I was forced to land and repair my pump.

I landed at the back of a forest close to a farm house; the district is unknown on account of the fog and the continuous changing of course.

I made preparations to set the machine on fire, but apparently was not observed, so was enabled to effect a repair, and continued at 3.15 am in a South Westerly direction after considerable difficulty in starting my engine single handed.

I tried several times to find my whereabouts by descending through the clouds, but was unable to do so. So eventually I landed and found out that it was at Cape Gris Nez, and took in some petrol. When the weather cleared I was able to proceed and arrived at the Aerodrome about 10.30 am.

As far as could be seen the colour of the Airship was green on top and yellow below and there was no machine gun or platform on top.

I have the honour to be, Sir,
Your obedient servant.
R A J Warneford.
Flt Sub-Lieutenant.'

In this the official report Rex made no mention of his arrest by the French.

A busy scene by the hangars. Just below the engine of Rex's Morane is one of only two Sopwith Gordon Bennett racers, No 1214, this example being essentially a modified Tabloid, with a 100hp Gnome rotary engine.

The heroes relax. From left: Sub Lt R S Mills, Sqn Cdr A W Bigsworth, Lt J P Wilson and Sub Lt R A J Warneford at St Pol.

He was not alone in destroying enemy aircraft that night. Wilson and Mills got home before him, and the station had been congratulating them on their successful attack on Zeppelins in their sheds at Evere. For this both pilots were awarded the Distinguished Service Cross. Fitter Albert Hawkins described how modest Rex was concerning his part in the destruction of the airship: on the day after the raid, when he had given his report to the CO he was asked to step out in front of the crews lined up to congratulate him. He just stood there for a moment, murmured his thanks, and said he had only done what any of them would have done in the same circumstances, and made a bolt for the hangar to see what state his Morane was in.

Time dragged for him in the next 24 hours. He was not allowed to fly, and when he was not with the Morane in the shed had to watch enviously the planes taking off, disappearing into the sky, and returning when their various missions were completed. In the evening he went down to the *Empress* at Dunkirk, and went to sleep. He had been called to the CO's office earlier and told that his immediate plans had been changed. Before going to London to be awarded the Victoria Cross by His Majesty King George V, he was to go to Paris where he would be given the Cross of the Legion of Honour.

Wing Commander Longmore was determined to keep Rex on his 'lap of honour' as long as possible, and there was no chance of Rex returning to ordinary life as a flier, until all the pomp and circumstance had died down. 'I cannot help wondering' said Longmore, 'how long it will be before young Warneford kills himself when he does come back to us'.

For the Germans the night of June 6th had been a major setback to their confidence concerning the vulnerability of their airships. Their High Command issued orders to their press, and that of the occupied countries, to suppress all news that would have an adverse effect on the morale of their people, but in spite of all the censorship, the information leaked out through many devious channels. The *Handels Blad* of Amsterdam on June 15th, referring to the attack by Wilson and Mills on the sheds at Evere, confirmed the rumour that an airship was totally destroyed on the ground, and that seven railway wagons filled with the wrecked framework of the Zeppelin were sent back to Germany. The *Tyd*, and the *Telgraf* of Amsterdam were also full of dramatic accounts of the destruction of the LZ37, and LZ38, even though the Germans commanded the Ghent newspapers to publish a report that all Zeppelins had returned safely to their bases on the night of June 6th. The townspeople of Ghent of course knew better, for they had personally witnessed the conflagration of the Convent of St. Elisabeth.

Soon fragments of the wreck were circulated among the people of Ghent and further afield. One of them turned up as a paperweight on the desk of the First Lord of the Admiralty, Mr Winston Churchill. A paragraph from a Belgian newspaper throws light on another unusual commodity, 'Zeppelin rings'.

'Some of the aluminium sections of the wreck have been secured by an enterprising merchant, and as a result what are known as Zeppelin rings are being sold in many parts of Belgium and worn openly by patriots in spite of threats of reprisal on any person caught wearing them. The rings have even found their way across the Channel to England. A nice gift for young ladies!'

A later report in the same paper said, 'At 2.30am on June 7th an attack was made on the airship sheds at Evere, north of Brussels. Bombs were dropped on the sheds which were observed to be in flames. These reached to a great height, and it was presumed that Zeppelins were burning inside. We have now heard that one has been destroyed, beside complete destruction of the fitting and repair departments. Both aeroplanes taking part in the attack managed to reach their bases safely.' Despite the German ban, everyone soon knew the real truth.

15

Paris

Rex was now a national hero in France as well as England, and after several days of official presentations at St Pol airfield he was ordered to Paris by Wing Commander Longmore. There he was to receive his Knight's Cross of the Legion of Honour, for which General Joffre had recommended him on June 9th, and was to attend other functions and celebrations. After that he would return to duty, collecting a new aircraft for the squadron and flying it back to St Pol.

Flight Lieutenant M S Marsden was with Rex during the few days he spent in Paris, and wrote an account of what happened:

'I was near Paris at the time he returned from Dunkirk, after his great achievement of shooting down the Zeppelin. Longmore sent me a chit asking me to keep an eye on young Warneford during his sojourn in Paris, as he had quite a programme ahead of him. I was at Coublay awaiting the delivery of a Nieuport when he was flown in. I was delighted to see him again. When he flew in at Coublay a civic welcome has been laid on; there was a celebration dinner, and he was toasted in the Mess. He was made to recount his encounter with the LZ37, and made a very good speech. He was extremely modest, saying it was all in the day's work ... or night's (cheers!) and that anyone who had the luck could have done the same thing.

'Later that evening we got a taxi-cab and set off for our billet in Paris. This happened to be the Ritz Hotel where another reception was the order of the day. There was a small crowd waiting to get a glimpse of Rex in spite of the late hour. He was cheered as we got out of the cab and went up the steps.

'When we managed to get rid of the officials who had been detailed to look after us, we had a chance to survey our accommodation. We had certainly been given the full treatment. Our suite consisted of two separate rooms, each with a bathroom, and a luxurious drawing-room. The tables in there were banked with flowers, surrounded by several bottles of champagne in buckets of ice. They must have imagined that we were going to celebrate through the night. We were too tired for that, and contented ourselves by riffling through the neat piles of telegrams, invitations and even envelopes containing photographs of beautiful mademoiselles who wished to make Rex's acquaintance.

'After we had managed to read some of the letters, (those in French rather foxed us) Rex was all for returning to Coublay as soon as possible. I succeeded in preventing him from making any such move, pointing out that it would be discourteous to our French hosts not to go through with the whole programme that

*After the victory: ground crew pose proudly
with the Morane at St Pol aerodrome.*

had been laid on. It might cause some complications if he did not appear at the military and civic receptions which had been arranged in his honour.'

Lieutenant Marsden accompanied Rex to the Ministry of Marine on Saturday June 12th, and there Monsieur Alexandre Millerand, Minister of War, who had taken a particular interest in military aviation since his appointment in 1912, pinned on Rex's tunic his own insignia as Chevalier of the Legion of Honour. Marsden continues: 'As the Minister kissed him on both cheeks he said in English, "I shall be proud to wear the one destined for you in its stead".

'We were escorted to the Opera, where everyone in the audience stood up and the orchestra played the British national anthem as we entered our box. Rex stood to attention and when the anthem was finished he waved and saluted them and was cheered in return. It was a very moving experience.

'We were obliged to go everywhere in uniform. It was very hard on them as our wardrobes were very meagre. The valets at the Ritz did their best with them. One of our difficulties was managing to preserve our brass buttons from too-enthusiastic souvenir hunters. Our togs were really more suited to the airfields than to the company of beautifully gowned and jewelled women and elderly diplomats in full evening dress. Even the young officers in Paris wore very smart dress uniforms on these social occasions. But I do not think that our appearance worried us in the least.

'It was handshakes, flowers, autograph hunters, gorgeous girls and champagne all the way. It was just as well that neither of us took advantage of all these diversions. Rex was a very abstemious drinker and seldom finished his glass. This he managed to do without offending his hosts in the least, which says something for his tact, as they were very pressing.'

About midday on Monday 14th Rex was whisked off to lunch with the British Ambassador, Sir Francis Leveson Bertie, and the Naval Attaché, Captain Michael H Hodges. After lunch the Ambassador took Rex upstairs to visit the wife of Lord Algernon Gordon-Lennox, a Colonel on General French's staff. Lady Algernon wrote about the meeting in her diary and after Rex's death included a copy of the entry in a letter to his mother:

'After luncheon Sir Francis brought him up to my sitting-room, and he and I had a long talk lasting about two hours. Such an attractive boy — so modest about his great achievement, and giving one an impression of carelessness and determination which are quite remarkable. He gave me a different version of anything I have seen in the papers ... Imagine going to sleep exhausted when he got back, and to be awakened and told there was a telegram from the King awarding him the Victoria Cross. When he was called to his Commanding Officer's office he thought that he was in for a rocket not an award. He talked about his childhood in India, and of the shipwreck at the time that war was declared: and always we got back to the same theme of destiny. Looking back on it now, it almost seems that I can hear him say: "It is all written, and I have no fear." I went with him to the lift, and as I pressed the button to send it down, his laughing boyish face looked up as he said: "Goodbye; *this* may be death, you know!" Three days later they brought me the news that he had been killed.'

'Each morning we were visited by a sort of major-domo,' Marsden remembers, 'who was detailed to be our guide-interpreter throughout our stay. As soon as we had had our breakfast he appeared and read out a typed itinerary of the day's engagements and invitations. These were so numerous that we were obliged to refuse more than we accepted. There was hardly a moment of the days and most of the nights which was not filled.

'We used to lie in as late as we dared in the mornings, talking into the intercom telephone beside our beds and swapping stories of the previous day's experiences. On the whole Rex found it "quite good fun", but he was always longing to get away and explore Paris without the insistent crowds. But we seldom managed to escape for a minute, as our kind hosts would not relinquish their hospitable grip.

'Early in our stay a very beautiful woman sent up her card to our suite, and suggested taking us for a drive around the sights of Paris. Her magnificent limousine, a Hispano-Suiza, stood outside the doors of the Ritz. She was the well-known society hostess, and France's first lady pilot, the Baroness de Laroche. It was plain to see that from the moment she set eyes on Rex she was very attracted to him. For his part I had always noticed how unconcerned he was about the opposite sex. Beyond casual girl-friends, he had always managed to evade any permanent attachments. All the time I knew him he was happiest on his own, though at all times with me a most delightful companion. I do not think any of us ever really broke through his reserve. But in the case of the Baroness it was a little bit different. He treated her from the beginning with more of a relaxed confidence than I had ever seen before. As the days passed she was more and more by his side. Her beautiful motor car was at our disposal, complete with her smart chauffeur in his dark green livery which matched the car.

'We usually went out together, but on one occasion Rex went along to her Paris house in the Rue St Honoré to have supper with her. For the first time in his life, I should say, he was in love. She was utterly charming with him. I think that people could not help noticing that they only had eyes for each other. But when we were alone together Rex never mentioned her name, so I, respecting his wish for silence on the subject, did not press him about his feelings.'

(Raymonde de Laroche was born at Paris on August 22nd 1886. She was taught to fly by Charles Voisin and Leon Delagrange in 1909 and 1910, and received her brevet, No36, from the Aero Club of France on March 8th 1910, becoming France's first woman pilot of heavier-than-air machines. She appeared at many of the great aviation meetings of the time: St Petersburg, Budapest, Rouen and Rheims. Despite a serious accident at Rheims in 1910 she was flying again in 1911, and was awarded the medal of the Legion of Honour, the first time it had been given to a woman pilot. Very soon women pilots were sufficiently numerous to have a special award, the Coupe Fémina, instituted for them, and Raymonde de Laroche won this on two occasions. After the war she specialized in high altitude flights and on June 17th 1919 she broke the women's altitude record with a flight of 3,900 metres. When this was surpassed by an American, Miss Ruth Law, who reached 4,270 metres, the Baroness de Laroche immediately responded with a new record of 4,800 metres. This was the crowning glory of her career, for, while training for a new Coupe Fémina competition, she was accidentally killed, together with Mlle Barrault, at Crotoy on July 18th 1919.)

The Baroness Raymonde de Laroche. The studio portrait which she gave to Rex during his visit to her home in Paris, and which was eventually returned to England with his personal effects.

Rex, proudly wearing his Cross of the Legion of Honour, poses outside the Ritz Hotel, Paris.

As the few days drew to their close, the adulation increased. The Paris crowds, sensing that they were about to lose their hero, became almost hysterical. Rex's right hand was strained by the clasping, and more than once he was seen to nurse his wrist as though it ached. In the streets an escort of gendarmes was detailed to prevent his being mobbed. Wherever he walked there seemed to be a forest of outstretched arms. It was a rather alarming experience, but through it all Rex maintained a calm exterior, though he must have been sorely tried at times, and he did not enjoy this side of his visit. His image was submerged in a sea of worship which had strained and broken the bounds of reality.

On the evening of Wednesday June 16th there was a final celebration of the honour that had been conferred on him. An article in the Paris paper *Le Soir* reported the event. 'In an elegant restaurant in the suburbs of Paris, friends and admirers of Flight Lieutenant Warneford entertained the aviator in celebration of his decoration of the Victoria Cross and the Legion of Honour for his act in destroying a Zeppelin near Ghent. The meal was drawing to a close when one of the most venerable and distinguished representatives of the French nobility approached his table, and in a few well chosen, most moving words, congratulated the young aviator. Lieutenant Warneford, who speaks French with difficulty, stammered out some words of thanks in his native tongue. One of the Englishmen present translated them, and when he was about to conclude, the young hero, rising to his feet, interrupted the speaker and in a loud voice cried, "Vive la France! Vivent les Alliés! et à bas le Boche!" and sat down blushing with embarrassment. The whole room greeted him with ringing cheers.'

Marsden recalled that later Rex was left in peace. 'Four of us remained at our table in the restaurant; myself, the Baroness, another girl, and Rex. The small orchestra was still playing and the lights were low. Most of the other diners had gone. I looked up, sensing that someone wished to give us a message. It was the cigarette girl. She was standing just behind Rex, and in her tray was a bunch of red roses, full-blown and wilting from the heat of the room. "Pour vous, Monsieur," she said holding them out to Rex. He stood up and took them from her, and as he held them their crimson petals slowly began to fall, one by one, over the cross of the Legion of Honour on the breast of his tunic. As they fell the girl burst into tears, ashamed that her gift was composed of faded flowers. Stammering her regret in broken English she said: "I brought them to wish you happiness when you go back to England". Taking her hand Rex replied: "Mademoiselle, thank you for your flowers; but they will be for my grave, for I shall not reach England. I will not live to see England again."

'When we got back to the Ritz, Rex was in a strange mood; whether it was an anti-climax after all the various hectic events I shall never know. He was reluctant to go to his room although the hour was very late. He sat on the edge of my bed, smoking innumerable cigarettes, and talked and talked. He spoke about India, his short school days, his grandfather, of whom he was very fond; of his years at sea; very briefly of his mother — "she was beautiful" — his sisters, his terrier Vic who was lost overboard in a gale at sea; and last of all about his father, of whom I had never heard him speak before. "He took me for rides in the jungle on elephants when he was building the railway, the Cooch Behar railway." I had never heard of it, but his father had built it, and that was enough for Rex. "I would like to have built something like that," he said, "something lasting and useful, something which really justifies one's existence."

'Rex never thought anything of his achievement in bringing down the LZ37. "That was just routine and over in a flash. But building a railway, that was something," and then, sadly, "I wish that I had never shot it down over the convent."

'At last he took himself off to bed, apologizing for keeping me up. He turned at the door to put out the light, and said wistfully: "I seem to have lost touch with reality these last few days, I hardly know who I am any longer." Was all this a premonition of his death the next day? It was the last talk I had with him, and in the morning we went our separate ways.'

Rex seated in the cockpit of a Henry Farman F22. Possibly taken on the day of his arrival in Paris.

16

Come, Winged Death

Rex slept rather late, and in the morning his mood seemed to have changed, for when he passed Marsden on his way to breakfast he said that he had never felt better. He drank his coffee and ate his buttered roll in the dining-room of the Ritz alone except for a waiter who served him.

He was now about to return to duty, for he had his instructions from Wing Commander Longmore to fly back to Dunkirk a new Henry Farman biplane for the squadron after first giving it an acceptance test at Buc aerodrome just outside Paris. Longmore had warned him that this new machine was not to be used for aerobatics such as Rex was accustomed to perform in his Morane.

The check-out flight, however, would not be completely straightforward, for the French authorities had taken the opportunity to grant a request from the American Ambassador that a leading American magazine writer should be given permission to make a flight over Paris in order to get material for a story. The writer, Henry Beach Needham from Wyncote, Pennsylvania, was at this time a freelance journalist, having previously worked for the New York Evening Post, among other publications. He had also been appointed by President Roosevelt to the important position of Housing and Labour Commissioner for the Panama Canal Zone in 1908.

Now, since the outbreak of war in Europe he had been travelling through Germany and Switzerland, as many other neutral correspondents did at the time, writing and sending his articles home. After Prague he had journeyed to London where he interviewed Lloyd George, among others, before moving to France. In his endeavour to see the war from both sides he had been pressing for permits to visit the war zone and certain other important areas. A request to visit Sir John French's headquarters at St Omer had been turned down, and he had then gone to Paris where he applied to the French military authorities for permission to accompany Monsieur Poincaré, the French President, on his next tour of the battle front. This was also refused, probably because of suspicions arising from his earlier visit to Germany. At this time the Germans were often generous with permission for visits to neutral journalists who showed any sympathy for their cause, and this would weigh heavily against a man like Needham among the spy-conscious allies. He was therefore preparing to sail back to America from Cherbourg on June 18th, but was finally granted a request to meet the Zeppelin hero, Rex Warneford, for an interview and a short flight over Paris, which the authorities must have considered harmless enough.

Rex met Needham for lunch on June 17th and probably gave him over the meal the desired interview, which would never be published. When he was leaving the Ritz on his way to this luncheon he was stopped by an English journalist who had been taking an interest in Mr Needham's activities. He was a correspondent for the *Graphic*, who afterwards said:

'On Thursday, June 17th, on calling at the Ritz, I found a friend talking to a young officer in RNAS uniform and wearing the medal of the Legion of Honour who proved to be Lieutenant Warneford, VC. I spoke to him about the Zeppelin, respecting which he said that he had done no more than any other airman given the same chance would have done. He mentioned that he was flying that afternoon, and that he was to take an American journalist up for a flight. He said that he did not like the idea. I asked him, "Why do it, then?" and he replied, "I cannot help myself ... I am bound to do it." He made several more remarks with the tacit understanding that they were not for repetition. He appeared to be in low spirits and added that he was tired of life. Then as I left, his face suddenly lit up with a charming smile and I was glad to see him in good spirits again and asked him if he would dine with me that night. He agreed, but all at once I saw that his face had clouded over. Calling there that night, I heard of his tragic end.'

After this meeting Rex went on to the lunch with Needham, who was no doubt much more enthusiastic about the coming flight than his pilot, especially as it was the result of the only one of his requests to be granted recently. Afterwards Rex went back to the Ritz again to meet someone who had only very recently made his acquaintance.

This was a young Naval Lieutenant, Robert Francis FitzGibbon, attached to HMS *President* for Miscellaneous and Special Services, but at that time officially on leave in Paris with his American-born wife Georgette. Like Rex they were staying at the Ritz, and after seeing him once or twice, FitzGibbon had arranged to accompany Rex on the trip to Buc. Now that Lieutenant Marsden was going to Villa Coublay to test a Nieuport and Rex had to go on his own to Buc with the American journalist, he may have been glad to find in FitzGibbon someone whom he could regard as a companion for a while rather than just another in the unending stream of admirers.

When Rex went upstairs to call for Lieutenant FitzGibbon as arranged, he discovered that Mrs FitzGibbon would be left alone when they had gone, so he asked her to come along as well, which she did. Then all three drove to the RNAS headquarters in the Avenue Montaigne where they picked up Mr Needham and went on to Buc.

Rex took Lieutenant FitzGibbon for his promised flight, which was short and uneventful, but by this time the weather was beginning to change. Dark clouds piled up in the west and the warm air grew chilly. People on the airfield turned up their collars as the wind rose slightly and little eddies of dust whirled about. According to some press reports, Mr Needham who was standing by the Farman aircraft looked up at the sky and remarked to a bystander that the weather was breaking.

Rex, who was still in his cockpit, asked him to hurry up and get in. Having made his test flight he was anxious to get the journalist's trip over. One of the ground staff

Above: Henry Beach Needham.

Left: Illustration of the crash based on a sketch by the 'Graphic' artist. This shows a Farman F22, not the F27 type.

Robert Francis Dillon FitzGibbon, 1884-1954.
Later known as R F FitzGibbon Lee-Dillon, he also had the French title of Comte de Dillon.
(Reference 'Dillon' in Burke's Peerage).

helped Mr Needham into the nacelle, and when he started to fiddle with the safety strap it was suggested that he need not bother with it if he found it awkward, as they would not be up for long.

Someone swung the propeller and the engine re-started with a roar. Just as the plane began to taxi, a man appeared, running fast across the grass, shouting and waving his arms. Rex did not notice him: the machine rolled more quickly along the strip, bouncing a little, and rose rapidly into the air. The man shrugged his shoulders and turned away. No one ever discovered who he was, and what message he was supposed to give, or to whom.

Then a long green limousine drew up by the airfield gates, and Raymonde de Laroche stepped out. Ever since Rex's strange announcement in the restaurant the previous night she had felt disturbed and worried that something was going to happen to him. She might have made up some excuse to try to stop him flying, although she must have known that it would be to no avail. But by now she was too late for that. Her car had been held up by military traffic on the roads around Paris, and she could only stand, shading her eyes as she looked up into the darkening sky where the aeroplane was circling.

At 2,000 feet Rex banked to start his landing approach, or so it seemed to those watching below. Suddenly the plane began to go into a spin. It dived steeply, then pulled out and appeared to fling up its tail which, with a crack that was heard on the ground, snapped off and caught the propeller, shearing part of it away. The machine started to roll, and at about 700 feet it turned upside-down. To the horror of the watchers, both occupants, neither apparently strapped in, fell one after the other to the ground, followed by the crippled aeroplane.

It had passed beyond the airstrip and fallen into a field of growing corn. Almost everyone on the airfield rushed to the spot. They reached Henry Needham first. He was dead, and lay half on his side, clutching a piece of light cane which had been part of his seat. Rex lay fifty feet away on his face. As they turned him over they could see that although he was still breathing he was unconscious and terribly injured. The insignia of the Legion of Honour had been driven through his tunic deep into his left side.

The airfield ambulance was quickly on the scene, and Rex was carefully placed in it on a stretcher. Raymonde was still standing by her car as the ambulance passed her. She got in and told her chauffeur to follow it. Her worst fears had been realized, and she felt that there was no hope for Rex's life.

The two vehicles made the best speed they could along the crowded roads to the British Military Hospital in the Trianon Palace Hotel at Versailles. On the way they passed a car carrying Lieutenant Marsden in the opposite direction. Having tested the Nieuport he had returned to the Ritz to collect his things. There he learnt of the crash and immediately set off for Buc in a fast car to see what had happened. Suddenly he saw, in the green car he knew so well, Raymonde sitting ashen-faced without recognizing him. He had his car turned round to follow the others.

He arrived at the hospital almost at the same time as Raymonde, and saw Rex being taken from the ambulance and wheeled inside on a trolley. While a doctor was being called, Lieutenant Marsden and Raymonde stood looking down at Rex. Marsden wrote later: 'I do not know if he knew we were there. As we stood helplessly looking, he gave a little sigh and opened his eyes. For less than a second he looked straight at me, almost as though he was going to make a sign that he knew us. Then his head turned away, and before the orderlies had wheeled him out of our sight he died.

'I took Raymonde home and left her with her maid, whom I told to phone the doctor. The whole tragedy was so extraordinary, so inexplicable, that I knew it would haunt us for the rest of our lives.'

Someone else who would remember that day for a long time was Georgette FitzGibbon, who had actually witnessed the crash. She wrote a letter to Rex's mother giving her recollection of what had happened.

Hotel Ritz, Paris

Dear Mrs Corkery,

It having been my privilege to spend the last afternoon of his life with your son ... I am writing to tell you the details as best I can... I had never seen your son before that afternoon when he came to take my husband, who is in the Navy, out to Buc where he was to take an aeroplane out to test it, for his first experience in flying, and when he saw that I was to be left alone for the afternoon he kindly asked me if I would go out with them and see him take my husband up. We went first to the Headquarters of the RNAS in a taxi, and there we changed in to a Naval motor and proceeded to Buc.

On the front seat was the American journalist who was with your son when the accident occurred. Driving through the streets your son was repeatedly recognised by officers of all ranks, and saluted by them all, and we felt proud of being with him. He was in very good spirits and laughed, and talked, and joked the whole journey ... He looked so well and so handsome that I do wish you had seen him. He described a good deal of his experiences in the most simple and natural and unaffected way.

When we arrived at Buc he had the Farman Biplane brought out at once. He told us how flying in a Farman was just like sitting on a sofa in the drawing room; it was so unexciting and even boring. What he liked was one of the fast Nieuport machines, where there was some excitement to be had, and you could go along at 80 or 90 miles per hour. I am telling you this so you can see there was no question of his nerves being shaken, and indeed I noticed every time he looked at me that I had never seen anyone with brighter or clearer eyes; they were like a child's.

He took my husband up for a short flight of a few minutes and then he landed and took up the American as a passenger. They had only been in the air a few minutes, and were circling and coming direct towards us, not at all high in the air, when suddenly the accident occurred. Experts say the propeller broke. Whatever it was that caused it, it was all over in a few moments, and there could have been no time for either of them to realize what was happening ...

Most sincerely yours,
Georgette FitzGibbon.

Even the eyewitnesses seemed unable to agree on the probable cause of the crash, and people cast about for something that would resolve the uncertainty. Various speculations were current in the press for a while, attributing the accident to

The wreckage of the Henry Farman F27 some hours after the fatal incident. The nacelle, with pusher engine to the left, is in the foregound. Behind this on the rudder can be seen the factory construction number, HF18.

anything from excess of alcohol or foolhardiness to sabotage or a hidden flaw in the scarcely tried aircraft.

At the official inquiry it was suggested that Lieutenant Warneford was coming in to land too high. To lose height he dived the machine too steeply, and pulled up too hard. Under the strain the right wing went back and broke. With the propeller smashed by part of the tail, and the engine still running, it was impossible to prevent disaster. The biplane itself was not completely destroyed, and it did not catch fire. Several of the instruments remained intact. The officers and staff at the aerodrome confirmed that Lieutenant Warneford was perfectly fit when he made the flight, and not suffering from fatigue or any other indisposition, and those who knew Rex or had flown with him said that it would not have been possible for him to make a bad mistake when landing. His landings were always reported as 'meticulous, even under severe conditions.'

Certain incidents were not fully reported, one of these being that an artist from the *Graphic* did make the journey out to the airfield at Buc. He saw the accident, and made a sketch of the men falling, and the diving aeroplane. This was used as the basis of a picture printed later in the *Daily Express*. Curiosity after speaking to Rex at the Ritz must have prompted him to go to the aerodrome to cover the story.

It was also thought by some who had been present that the man who ran out waving his arms and shouting as the plane took off was actually trying to stop the flight, but he never came forward at the inquiry.

Henry Needham died of multiple head injuries sustained, it was thought, when he was hit either by the propeller blade or by part of the wing. His body was eventually sent back to America for burial.

The post-mortem on Rex showed that there had never been the slightest chance of him surviving his injuries, which included a fractured skull, two broken arms, and a mass of fractures to the right leg and hip.

That Thursday evening the paper *Paris Soir* wrote: 'He who defied the storm has been killed by a breeze.'

17

Those Whom the Gods Love

'Heaven gives its favourites early death.' wrote the *Manchester Guardian*. 'There is a tragic irony about the death of Flight Lieutenant Warneford, which is new to the history of flight, strewn with tragedy as that history has been. His successful attack on the Zeppelin, on June 7th, which so fully earned him the Victoria Cross, was the most daring and picturesque exploit imaginable.

'The attention of the world, that has been almost bewildered by bravery, that has seen the highest instances of individual daring turned into the commonplace of a newspaper, was gripped at once. Men everywhere were thrilled by the sudden realization of an episode in aerial warfare which had hitherto only been seen in the works of imaginative writers and their illustrators. Now, after barely a fortnight since his great feat echoed round the world, the news of Lieutenant Warneford's death follows it.

'The man who dared all in a duel with a Zeppelin, and came safely through, has been killed while testing a new aeroplane of a particularly safe type. Though the fame can never be touched, the tragedy is deepened by the pitifully short interval between winning it, and the descent of "the blind Fury with the abhorred shears." Thomas Hardy, ever on the watch in his novels and poems for the mockery of the immortals, never conceived them in a more jealous mood.'

Violently as the news of the Zeppelin's destruction had assailed the front pages of the world, it could not compare with what was printed on Rex's death. Leading journalists vied with each other in writing extravagant obituaries, their every phrase describing and enlarging on the wounds inflicted by the arrows of misfortune upon a mourning nation.

The impact of his death was put to many uses, not the least of which was that of promoting and encouraging the recruiting drive. A report of London's reaction at the recruiting hut of the Sportsman's Battalion, outside the Hotel Cecil, states: 'The shining example of the young man who had joined the battalion only a few months ago has been a great asset to the recruiting. A large picture of the hero looks out with a sort of grim assurance from a prominent position on the wall of the hut. By the side of it are pinned the latest newspaper cuttings describing his end. Around it all day passed an ever-changing crowd. The recruiting sergeant had the easiest time of his career as he went among them appealing to old as well as young "... not to let young Warneford be the last of the heroes of the Sportsman's Battalion."

'Along the hoardings which conceal the demolished site of the old Tivoli is a

gallery of pictures from the papers extolling Warneford's exploit. Men pause to look at them, and before they know where they are, the bulky form of the sergeant, like a fat spider, is between them and the pictures, and as likely as not they follow him meekly into his little den behind the pots of geraniums, to sign on for a shilling.'
— It seemed that stark tragedy was an incentive to join the colours.

On Friday, June 18th, Rex's body was laid out in the mortuary of the Versailles military hospital, which had been transformed into a *chapelle ardente*. The most lovely roses and other flowers had been gathered by the nurses, medical staff and convalescent soldiers, and placed around the coffin which was covered with a Union Jack. Two British soldiers stood at the end of the catafalque with their rifles reversed; they were relieved at intervals during that day and night. Floral tributes continued to arrive in a steady stream, one in particular being a massive aeroplane composed entirely of red and white roses. On its left wing was a replica of the Victoria Cross, and on the right the Cross of the Legion of Honour. The propeller was made of white roses tied with a ribbon bearing the inscription: 'Honoured by the King, admired by the Empire, but mourned by all.' Extra police were needed to control the large band of mourners who wished to file past the coffin and pay their respects.

It was originally intended to hold a simple funeral service in the hospital chapel, and an interment afterwards in the hospital grounds. This plan had already been put into operation: a contingent from the Royal Naval Air Service had been detailed to attend the funeral and Albert Hawkins, who had always serviced Rex's aircraft at St Pol, had asked to be included among the pall bearers when, all of a sudden, this programme was countermanded. Rex's body was to be sent back to England for a public funeral. The press of both England and France now indulged in an orgy of articles for and against the idea. Controversies grew out of all proportion to the sadness and dignity of the occasion.

Finally, on Monday June 21st, at 5.30am, a motor hearse glided out through the iron gates of the British hospital and made its solitary way to the St Lazare railway station, where it was met by eight British flying men from Buc aerodrome who had been detailed to accompany the coffin to Dieppe. The train stood unnoticed on a siding, the proceedings having been kept secret on special orders issued by the French military authorities. There was to be no public leave-taking. None of Rex's squadron from St Pol had permission to attend. Lieutenant Marsden was engaged upon his flying duties at Coublay: Fitter Hawkins' request to act as a bearer was disregarded.

The train was shunted alongside the main platform as soon as the coffin had been carried into the funeral coach, and the doors closed and sealed. The passengers, who knew nothing of Rex's proximity, took their seats for their various destinations. At 8.55am the whistle blew, the guard dropped his flag and slowly the long train moved out into the sunshine, gathering speed on its way through the French countryside towards the coast.

On the quayside at Dieppe detachments of Belgian, French, and English troops formed a guard of honour as the coffin, protected in a flag-draped crate, was hoisted on board ship. During the voyage across the Channel it rested on the port side of the ship. When the last passenger had disembarked at Folkestone the bearer party shouldered their burden and placed it in a van directly behind the engine of the waiting train, with many of the wreaths and the floral aeroplane being loaded into a second van.

England, her people's sympathies whipped to near hysteria by the extravagant funeral orations of the national press, awaited the homecoming of her dead hero. The streets around Victoria station were crowded fully an hour before the train was due. Shortly before it pulled in the gates to the platform were closed, and nobody except two of Rex's sisters and a few officials was allowed through. The doors of the van were opened, and in silence Rex's coffin was raised by eight leading seamen of the Royal Naval Division who bore it to a waiting gun-carriage in the station yard. Twenty blue-jackets took up the ropes, and the Union Jack was replaced by a larger flag. Rex's cap rested on the head of the coffin beside a small spray of roses and laurels which bore no card. Wreaths from his mother and sisters, as well as the aeroplane of roses, were arranged round the coffin.

At 9.00pm the procession drew out of the station yard. There was no music, only the crisp voices of the officers giving short commands, and the muffled tramp of marching feet on the wooden blocks of the streets. Crowds lined the way, many of them not knowing what it was all about. As the cortège proceeded slowly west, the fading twilight of summer's longest day spread a rose-coloured glow over the land. Several hundred people walked behind, forming another procession down Buckingham Palace Road, through Chelsea, along the Embankment and into Fulham Road. A girl standing with her soldier boy-friend outside Burton Court was heard to remark: 'How sad to die when he had done all that.' 'How sad,' replied the soldier 'had he died before.'

The gates of Brompton Cemetery opened to allow the cortège through, then closed with a clang before the mass of spectators could enter. The last thing that the people could see, as they pressed close to the bars of the gates, was the gleam of the white roses on the wings of the flowered aeroplane.

Rex's body lay that night in the annexe of the cemetery chapel. The funeral was to take place at 4.00pm the following day. Early in the afternoon of June 22nd, people began to flock to the cemetery, and look into the laurel and fern-lined grave. As the hour drew near this section was roped off, but the crowds on the north side were dense and deep. Large numbers of latecomers were refused admission and had to stand outside in the Fulham and Richmond roads.

Rex's mother and the few family mourners, various officers representing the Admiralty, the RNAS, the Royal Flying Corps, and the Armoured Car Section of the Naval Air Service took their seats in the chapel and the first part of the burial commenced. Two chaplains of the Royal Naval Division — the Rev. Hugh Stallard and the Rev. G H Hewitt — conducted the service.

At 4.10pm the chapel bell began to toll. Eight men of the Royal Naval Division raised the coffin to their shoulders and followed the clergy from the chapel. The coffin was placed on the gun-carriage and the procession moved off towards the grave, along an avenue lined by men of the Armoured Car Section and of the Royal Naval Division. Before the grave a firing-party of 50 men stood with arms reversed and bowed heads.

The prayers of committal to the earth were quietly read, the flag was drawn aside

Police and servicemen attempt to hold back the crowds swarming towards the graveside in Brompton Cemetery.

Rex's mother and sisters, flanked by a guard of honour, watch as the coffin is prepared after leaving the chapel.

and folded, and a simple wreath from Rex's mother was laid on the shining lid of the coffin in silence. Then it was lowered into the grave until it slowly passed from sight of all but those who stood very near. The firing-party was brought sharply to attention, their boots grating on the gravel walk. At a crisp command the rifles swung aloft as one. Three volleys rang out. A cloud of London pigeons catapulted into the sky, the fluttering of their wings mingling with the reverberations of the salute. As the echoes died away the men of the Naval Division with bayonets fixed presented arms, while the mourners and the crowd, bareheaded, stood for a few moments in reverent silence. Then the air was filled with the melancholy notes of the Last Post, as bugles sounded their poignant farewell: farewell to youth, to brave endeavour, to loneliness.

The mourners departed; the servicemen, including a party of Chingford trainees under the command of Flight Lieutenant Merriam, were marched off, and the empty gun-carriage was drawn quietly away. The crowds, drained of emotion, slowly dispersed, thousands of them passing by the grave to look at the coffin before it was covered. When at last there was no one left, two men in drab clothes moved aside the wreaths and began to fill the grave.

The pigeons came back to the tall trees to roost. In the chapel lay the withered floral aeroplane, the scarlet and white petals of its French roses scattered over the floor. Soon the cemetery regained its tranquil seclusion, and Rex was left in peace, close to the grave of one who would have been most proud of him, his dear grandfather Tom.

Later the moon came up, painting a silver pathway along the wide waters of the Thames; the moon which had guided the marauding Zeppelins to the heart of the city, and would again: but their might had been challenged by the young man who now lay deep in his flower-strewn grave. Old Count Zeppelin's belief that his airships were immune from attack from the air had been destroyed for ever.

Hush! For his heart, that knew not any fear
Is stilled for ever, and our praises fall
Upon deaf ears. He is no longer there
To spend himself, a splendid prodigal,
As the two crosses that the Nations gave
Will shine, not on his breast, but on his grave.

(Anon)

COURAGE
INITIATIVE INTREPIDITY

FLIGHT·SUB·LIEUT·REGINALD
ALEXANDER·JOHN·WARNEFORD
V.C·R.N.A.S·BORN·15·OCT·1891
ACCIDENTALLY·KILLED·17·JUNE·1915

ERECTED·BY·READERS·OF·THE·DAILY
EXPRESS·TO·COMMEMORATE·THE·HEROIC
EXPLOIT·IN·DESTROYING·A·ZEPPELIN
AIRSHIP·NEAR·GHENT·ON·JUNE·7·1915

Daily Express Memorial, Brompton Cemetery

Bibliography

The Warneford Family collection of letters, photographs, etc

Bacon, Sir Reginald *The Dover Patrol 1915-1917*, 2 vols Hutchinson, 1919

Buckland, C E *The Dictionary of Indian Biography* Sonnenschein, 1906

Creagh, Sir G O'Moore *The VC and DSO*, 3 vols Standard Art Book Co, 1924

Dudley, Ernest *Monsters of the Purple Twilight* Harrap, 1960

Elsmie, G R (ed) *Field Marshal Sir Donald Stewart* John Murray, 1903

Gamble, C F Snowden *The Story of a North Sea Air Station* Humphrey Milford, 1928

Jones, H A *The War in the Air*, vols II-III Oxford University Press, 1928-31

Longmore, Sir Arthur M *From Sea to Sky 1910-1945* Geoffrey Bles, 1946

Merriam, F Warren *First through the Clouds* Batsford, 1954

Morris, Joseph *The German Air Raids on Great Britain 1914-1918* Sampson Low, 1925

Neumann, G P *The German Air Force in the Great War* Hodder & Stoughton, 1921

Raleigh, Sir Walter A *The War in the Air*, vol I Oxford University Press, 1922

Rawlinson, Sir Alfred *The Defence of London 1915-1918* Andrew Melrose, 1923

Robinson, Douglas Hill *The Zeppelin in Combat* Foulis, 1962

Robinson, Douglas Hill *Giants in the Sky* Foulis, 1973

Roskill, S W (ed) *Documents relating to the Naval Air Service, vol I, 1908-1918:* Navy Records Society, 1969

Schmalenbach, Paul *Die Deutschen Marineluftschiffe* Koehler, Herford, 1977

Wilson, Herbert Wrigley *The Great War*, 13 vols Amalgamated Press, 1914-19

Zeppelin-Welfahrten vom ersten Luftschiff 1899... Bilderstelle Lohse, Dresden, 1933

The following sources were also consulted:

Cooch Behar State Papers; *Burke's Peerage; The Navy List;*

and various issues of the following periodicals:

Daily Express, Daily Graphic, Le Figaro, The Graphic, L'Illustration, Lloyd's List, The London Gazette, Le Matin, Sunday Express, The Times, Het Volk (Ghent), *The War Budget, Zig Zag* (Santiago de Chile).

Index

(Illustrations in bold type)

Aeroplane Types:
British
Avro 504, 60, 72, 75, **75**
Avro 504C, 74
Bristol biplane, 55
Short S81, 80
Sopwith Gunbus, 80, **81**
Sopwith Tabloid, 71, **72**
French
Blériot, 80
Henry Farman, **56**, 83, **83**, 84, 112, 116, **117**
Morane Saulnier L, **66**, 67, 83, 84, **84**, 87, 94, 95, **96**, **100**, **104-5**
Nieuport, **63**, **64**, 74, 113
Voisin, **56**, 65, **65**, 66, 67
German
Taube, 66
Airships:
British
NS11, 29
German
Army Airship Service, 71, 74
History, 70, 71
Naval Airship Division, 71
Raids on English coast, 53, 73, 74
Viktoria Luise, **70**
L3, L4, L6, L8, 73; *L9,* 82; *L70,* 71; *LZ37,* 74, 82, 83, 85, **86, 92,** 99, 102, 103, 111; *LZ38,* 74, **76,** 78-80, 82-84, 102; *LZ39,* 74, 75, 82, 83; *ZIX,* 72; *ZXII,* 73, 74
Andaman Islands, 11
Angamos Point, Chile, 44, 45
Antofagasta, Chile, 44, 45, 47

Babington, Flight Commander J T 72, 73
Banbury, Charles, 57
Banbury, Evelyn, 57-59
Banbury, Sir Frederick, 57
Barnes, Flight Lieutenant D M, 80, 81
Belfort, France, 72
Berchem Ste Agathe, Belgium, 71, 82, 83
Bigsworth, Flight Commander A W, **68,** 75, **75, 101**
Bertie, Sir Francis Leveson, 106
Briggs, Squadron Commander E F, 72, 73
British India Steam Navigation Co Ltd, 31, 35, 42

Brompton Cemetery, 35, 120, **121, 122,** 123
Buc, aerodrome, 112, 113, 116, 119
Buttlar Brandenfels, *Oberleutnant* Horst, *Freiherr* von, 73, 79

Calcutta, India, 11, 13, 17, 25, 30, 31
Callao, Peru, 43, 46, 49
Campbell, Captain Alexander, 13, 17, 23, 25, 35
Cannon, Flight Sub-Lieutenant R P, 72
Central Flying School, 53, 57, 59
Chimba Bay, Chile, 45
Churchill, Mr Winston Spencer, 52, 71 72, 80, 102
Cologne, 71, 72
Cognelée, Belgium, 71
Convent of St Elisabeth, Ghent, 89-93, **92**
Cooch Behar, India, 14, 20, 23, 27, 35
Cooch Behar, Maharajah of, 14, **15,** 19, 22
Cooch Behar, Railway, 14, 18, 19, 35, 110
Corkery, Captain M P, 24, 25, 35, 43
Coronel, battle of, 49
Coublay, France (ie Villa Coublay), 103, 113, 119
Cradock, Admiral Sir Christopher, 49
Cunliffe-Owen, Mrs E, 51, 97

D'Albiac, J H, 66
Darjeeling, India, 13, 18, 20, 22, 25, 34
Double Chance, horse, **85**
Dover Patrol, 62, 63
Dunkirk, 60, 61, 63, 64, 66
Düsseldorf, 71, 72

Eastchurch, Royal Naval Air Station, 53, 59, 60
'Eastchurch Squadron', 61, **61,**
Etterbeek, Belgium, 71
Evere, Belgium, 71, 78, 82, 83, 101

FitzGibbon, Mrs Georgette, 113, 116
FitzGibbon, Lieutenant Robert Francis Lee Dillon, 113, **114,** 116
Friedrichshafen, 71-73
Fritz, *Kapitänleutnant* Johann, 73
Fuhlsbüttel, Germany, 71, 73
Furnes, aerodrome, 84, 95

George V, 98, 99, 101
Gerrard, Squadron Commander E L, 60

Ghent, 87, 89
Gontrode, Belgium, 71, 87
Gordon-Lennox, Lady Algernon, 106
Graphic correspondent/artist, 113, **114**, 117
Grey, Squadron Commander Spenser D A, 71, 72, 74, 75
Groves, Commander R M, 55

Hage, Germany, 82, 83
Hacgen, *Oberleutnant* Otto von der, 82, 85, 87, **90**
Hawkins, Albert E, 63, **63**, 69, 99, 101, 119
Hendon, 53, 55, 57
Hewitt, The Rev G H, 120
Highworth, Wilts, 59
Hodges, Captain M H, Naval Attaché, 106

Ireland, Flight Commander W P de Courcy, 80

Joffre, General J J C, 103

Keats, John: *Sleep and Poetry*, 24, 68, 69
King Edward VI School, Stratford-upon-Avon, 27, 28, 30

Lagatos Bank, 44
Laroche, Baroness Raymonde de, 107, **108**, 110, 115, 116
Lehmann, *Kapitän* Ernst, 73
Linnarz, *Hauptmann* Erich, 74, 78, 79, 81, 83
London, air raid of May 31st, 1915, 78-81
London and Pacific Petroleum Co Ltd, 42, 49
Longmore, Wing Commander Arthur M, 62, 63, 65-68, **68**, 69, 83, 96, 99, 101-3, 112

Marix, Flight Lieutenant R L G, 71, 72
Marsden, Flight Lieutenant Michael S, 60, 68, 87, 89, 95, 103, 106, 107, 110, 112, 113, 115, 119
Masius, *Hauptmann*, 82
Mathy, *Kapitänleutnant* Heinrich, 82
Maubeuge, Belgium, 71, 73, 74
Meddis, Leading Mechanic G E, 66, 67, 75
Merriam, Flight Lieutenant F Warren, 55, 68, 80, 123

Millerand, Alexandre, 106
Mills, Flight Sub-Lieutenant J S, **68**, 83, 84, 101, **101**, 102
Morrison, Sub-Lieutenant J S, 80
Mühler, *Steuermann* Alfred, 85, 87, 89, 91
Mulock, Flight Sub-Lieutenant R H, 74

Needham, Henry Beach, 112, 113, **114**, 115-7
Nightingale, Maude (née Warneford), 11, 13, 29, 30, 43
Noble Roy, horse, 57
Nordholz, 71

Orchard Gallardo, salvage firm, 45

P & O Orient Lines, 25, 31, 34, 43
Pemberton Billing, Lieutenant N, 72
Pigg, Mr R A, 42
Platen Hallermund, *Kapitänleutnant* Magnus, *Graf* von, 73

Rawlinson, Colonel A, 80
Robertson, Flight Lieutenant A W, 80
Rose, Sub-Lieutenant, **68**, 83, 84
Royal Flying Corps, 52, 120
Royal Naval Air Service, 52, 53, 60, 61, 62, 64, 74, 83, 113, 119, 120
Royal Naval Division, 120, 123

St Pol, aerodrome, 61, **62**, 64, 74, 95, 96
Samson, Commander C R, 61, 62
Satley, Co Durham, 25, 27, 29
Sevenhampton, Wilts 57, 58
Ships: HMS *Adventure*, 82; HMS *Albion*, 64; HMS *Empress*, 63, 96, 99, 101; HMS *Formidable*, 53; HMS *Good Hope*, 49; HMS *Monmouth*, 49; HMS *President*, 113; HMS *Royal Edward*, 74; SS *Ekma*, 35; SS *Dwarka*, 36; SS *Itola*, 36; SS *Lalpoora*, 36; SS *Lama*, 36; SS *Lhasa*, 36; SS *Lindula*, 36; SS *Lusitania*, 97; SS *Mina Brea*, 42-49, **47**, **48**; SS *Nagoya*, **41**, 42; SS *Somali*, 31, **32**, 34, 35, 42; SS *Vadala*, 35; SS *Victoria*, 34
Simla, India, 20
Sippe, Flight Lieutenant S V, 72, 73
Sitwell, Squadron Commander, 55, **56**
Spee, Admiral *Graf* von, 49
Sportsman's Battalions, Royal Fusiliers, **50**, 51, 52, **97**, 118

Stallard, The Rev H, 120
Stewart, General Sir Donald, 11, 12, 13, 28, 35
Strasser, *Korvettenkapitän*, Peter, 71, 73

Talcahuano, Chile, 46, 49
Travers, Flight Sub-Lieutenant Ben, 60, 80, 81
Trianon Palace Hotel, 115

Upavon, Wilts, Central Flying School, 53, 57, 59

Versailles, military hospital, 115, 119
Villa Coublay (Coublay), 103, 113, 119

Walsh, Captain J T, 42, 44-46
Warneford, Alexandra (née Campbell, afterwards Corkery), 13, 14, 17, **17,** 18, 19, **19,** 20, 22-25, 35, 43, 110, 116, 120
Warneford, Charlotte, 14
Warneford, John Robert Kemys, 57, 64
Warneford, Katharine, 27, 29
Warneford, Reginald Alexander John: birth, 18; childhood, 20-22; separation of parents, 22-24; sent to England, 25-27, 28, **29,** 30; joins P&O, 31-34; naval career, 35-37, 42-49; hospital at Calcutta, 38-41; joins SS *Mina Brea*, 42; meeting with mother, 43; stranding of SS *Mina Brea*, 44, 45; enlists in Sportsman's Battalion, 51; transfers in RNAS, 52; training, 53, **54;** posted to Dunkirk, 60, **68;** destroys the *LZ37*, 83-96, **88, 96,** 99, 100, **101;** telegram from King George V, **98,** 99; visit to Paris, 101, 103-111, **109, 111;** accident and death at Buc, **114,** 115-117, **117;** funeral, 118-123, **121, 122**
Warneford, Reginald William Henry, 11-14, 17-23, **19,** 35, 68-9, 110
Warneford, The Rev Thomas Lewis, 11-13, 25-28, **26,** 30, 35, 123
Warneford, W K F G, 29
Warneford Place, 57-59, **59**
Wilson, Flight Lieutenant J P, **68,** 83, **85,** 101, 102

Zeppelin, Count Ferdinand von, 70, 123
Zeppelin rings, 102
Zeppelins, see Airships, German

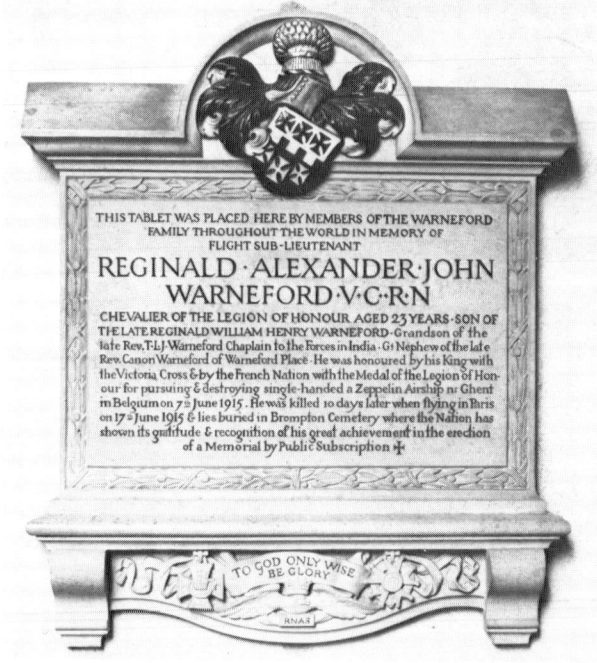

Memorial tablet in St Michael's Church, Highworth